The Silk Road and Black Death

An Enthralling Guide to the Routes That Connected Continents and the Event That Redefined Them

Free limited time bonus

Stop for a moment. We have a free bonus set up for you. The problem is this: we forget 90% of everything that we read after 7 days. Crazy fact, right? Here's the solution: we've created a printable, 1-page pdf summary for this book that you're reading now. All you have to do to get your free pdf summary is to go to the following website:

https://livetolearn.lpages.co/enthrallinghistory/

Once you do, it will be intuitive. Enjoy, and thank you!

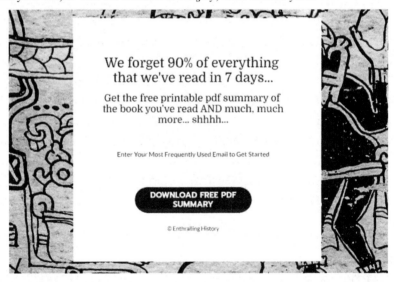

Table of Contents

Part 1: The Silk Road

An Enthralling Overview of the Ancient Trade Routes That Connected China to Europe

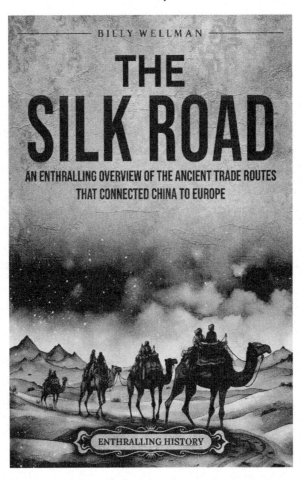

Introduction

Living in a world with the instant connectivity of the internet and the speed of modern travel makes it sometimes difficult to imagine what life was like thousands of years ago when the world was limited to what a person could reach by horseback near their home.

Not only was a person's travel limited, but their access to things like food, fabrics, and other supplies was restricted to whatever grew near them or what was created by people in their village. There was not a lot of variety in goods, and even the knowledge and religion that people experienced were limited since they rarely had the opportunity to come in contact with different cultures.

The Silk Road changed this way of life for multiple cultures all along the four-thousand-mile east-to-west trade route. Tradesmen carried goods, although far more than goods were spread from east to west and, in return, from west to east.

People in the West tasted tropical fruits from the East for the first time. The trade in spices revolutionized cooking around the globe. Religions spread from one region to the next. Scientific advancements began to happen as cultures put their ideas and resources together.

The Silk Road brought together pastoral and agrarian societies, uniting very different cultures from all over Eurasia and beyond with the trade of goods and the sharing of ideas.

The Silk Road also made many empires wealthy, thanks to the sale of goods and the taxes paid on items at ports of entry. Western empires and kingdoms lusted over luxury goods from the Far East, like silk and gemstones. Stories of journeys to exotic places along the Silk Road fueled imaginations for centuries and led to famous literary works.

What were the historical factors that inspired humans to trade with each other, though?

This book will break it down for you in simple terms. See how it began from the earliest points in history. Watch the rise and fall of the Silk Road alongside the rise and fall of empires. Find out who traveled the Silk Road and why, and gain insight into the fascinating impact the Silk Road had on everything in the world, from architecture to cooking.

What would life be like today if humanity had never begun trading along the Silk Road?

Chapter 1: The Silk Road: A Journey Through Time

Imagine a road that extends four thousand miles, spreads between three continents, and winds through some of the most intense and harrowing landscapes on Earth.

From the Yellow Sea in the east to the Mediterranean Sea in the west, the Silk Road was a network of pathways rather than a single road. These pathways connected the edges of Europe to East Asia, bringing together many cultures and societies that were vastly different from each other.

Travelers followed these trade routes through the Gobi Desert, where temperature extremes and the lack of water challenged caravans and where shifting sand threatened both humans and their goods. The Silk Road twisted through the freezing Himalayan Mountains, where brave travelers suffered from altitude sickness, bitter cold, and deadly avalanches, and traversed the grassy plains of the Eurasian Steppe.

Every turn of the Silk Road came with the possibility of death by nature or attack by roving bandits. In a time before planes, trains, and automobiles and in the days before vast sea trade routes were well established, the main source of transportation was horseback or camel caravan. The journey along the Silk Road was slow and arduous for travelers.

The Silk Road connected the countries and regions of China, central Asia, Persia (modern-day Iran), the Middle East, India, parts of East Africa, and the edges of Europe. The Mediterranean Sea was an important hub along the Silk Road, connecting the countries in Asia to Europe in the west. Major cities like the Egyptian city of Alexandria became trade hubs. Other important connecting cities were Constantinople, which is known today as Istanbul, and Antioch in Syria, which was a Greek city during the Hellenistic period.

The paths of the Silk Road were first worn smooth by the feet of people who carried goods for sale and trade. However, the Silk Road quickly became more than just a place where goods were transported. Along with the silks, spices, and dyes came the exchange of ideas, religions, art, traditions, and technologies as travelers interacted with different cultures and religions.

Cultural diffusion had almost as big of an impact on world history as the exchange of goods. In fact, the Silk Road's impact on world history was so powerful that it will be forever known as a bridge between civilizations and a testament to the strength of human collaboration across diverse cultures and long distances.

Despite being named the Silk Road in our modern history books, it was not actually a paved road or even a designated pathway in most areas. No one living along the Silk Road called it by this name. Instead, they would refer to it as the road to the next village or the road to a certain landmark up ahead. The unmarked paths of the Silk Road were made up of mountain passes, rivers, and deserts, and directions were given from one oasis or village to the next. Most people hired local guides to get them through each section of the road safely.

The Silk Road did not earn its official historical name until a German geographer by the name of Baron Ferdinand von Richthofen coined the phrase "the Silk Road" in 1877 when he used it in his atlas.

The Silk Road's popularity as a trade route spanned almost a millennium! It began in the 2nd century BCE and slowly faded away around the 15th century CE.

Let us take a quick look at the timeline of the Silk Road as its significance and use ebbed and flowed throughout various regions and throughout world history. With just a glance, you can see how the Silk Road was woven into many famous historical events and well-known time periods.

2nd Century BCE

What could have possibly motivated people to leave home and venture out on a dangerous journey along the Silk Road? To understand their motivations, we need to consider what life was like in the 2nd century BCE.

When the Silk Road was first becoming established, the Han dynasty ruled over China. The Chinese people were agrarian, which means they were farmers who cultivated the land. In the 2nd century BCE, China made the world-altering decision to more aggressively pursue trade with other people besides the nomads and nearby civilizations in central Asia.

Central Asia was populated with numerous tribes at this time. Chinese Emperor Wu Di sent out an exploratory mission to visit some of these tribes in an effort to officially establish trade. He sent his envoy Zhang Qian on the first journey along what would become known as the Silk Road. Zhang Qian's journey was filled with unexpected twists and turns, as he was captured by nomads and spent ten years in captivity before escaping and continuing on.

In the end, his journey was not only successful, but it also remains well known today since it significantly contributed to Chinese history. Zhang Qian gathered information about different cultures, regions, and routes and reported back to Emperor Wu Di, empowering him to make the necessary diplomatic connections in order to pave the way for friendly trade. This led to the development of the Silk Road and earned Zhang Qian the nickname "Father of the Silk Road."

1st to 2nd Century CE

The Roman Empire blazed onto the scene of history during the 1st century BCE. As you may know, the Roman Empire was powerful and ever expanding. The Romans also loved silk, and they developed an enjoyment of many other items from the Far East, including spices, gemstones, clothing, precious metals, and ivory. Fur, chemicals for curing leather, and paper were also popular trade items. Regular patterns of trade between the Roman Empire and the Far East began to solidify along the Silk Road during this time period.

The Roman Empire and the eastern Asian countries were so far apart that a single person could not travel the entire route alone. Trade was facilitated by a series of middlemen from tribes and regions all along the Silk Road. With these intermediaries, the sharing of cultural influences between regions began.

Want to know a lesser-known fact about the Silk Road? Silk was one of the many goods transported along the trade route, but arguably one of the most essential items was paper! Paper was invented in the East in the 1st century CE, although it would take a few centuries before it became a popular trade item on the Silk Road.

The earliest evidence of paper ever discovered is in the form of a written report addressed to Han Emperor Ho-di. It is dated to 105 CE.[1] From there, paper spread along the earliest routes of the Silk Road through China. Papers dating back to the 2nd century CE have been found in the cities of Loulan, Kotan, Kusha, and Dunhuang.

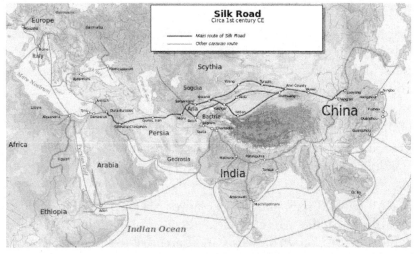

The Silk Road in the 1st century CE.

4th to 5th Centuries CE

The world roared right along into the 4th century CE. The paths of the Silk Road were becoming well traveled by this point in time; well, that is until a hiccup occurred. When the Western Roman Empire faced collapse, the demand for luxury items from the Far East plummeted.

6th to 7th Centuries CE

Nevertheless, the Silk Road stayed busy. The Byzantine Empire continued to grow in importance during the 6th century CE, and it established itself as an essential intermediary in the trade between the East and the West along the Silk Road, sharing its culture and art along with its merchandise.

---

[1] http://www.silk-road.com/artl/papermaking.shtml/

7th to 8th Centuries CE

The Chinese Tang dynasty peaked in the East during this period. At the same time, the Islamic caliphates were busy making all kinds of connections, further adding to the Silk Road and turning it into a web of pathways. The Silk Road was now large enough to connect the Mediterranean cities, central Asia, and China.

13th Century CE

Fast forward in time. Everything had been humming along quite smoothly. Trade along the Silk Road for the last few centuries had been magnificent. In fact, trade continued to build relationships between groups of people who would otherwise have nothing in common.

During the 13th century, a ruthless player in history rose to power and established his territory over a large part of the Silk Road. You may have heard of him before. His name was Genghis Khan of the Mongol Empire. He was followed by another famous Mongolian name in history, Kublai Khan.

The Mongol Empire held control over a key part of the Silk Road, linking China to the Mediterranean Sea.[2] Though the Mongols were known for their military conquests and fierce battle strategies, the Mongol Empire was also responsible for a key peace called the Pax Mongolica, which lasted from the 13th to the 14th century. The Pax Mongolica brought peace between different cultures and territories along the Silk Road, allowing trade to flourish because of the safety and stability that could be found in the region.

The Mongols also developed a type of postal system called the Yam. This helped information and trade goods move along the routes of the Silk Road and through all Mongolian territories more easily and efficiently, providing excellent opportunities for growth, both economically and in their administration.

Although the Mongols are often remembered as brutal warriors, many of their leaders had diplomatic tendencies and promoted cultural tolerance. For instance, Kublai Khan was interested in academia and the arts. He encouraged the translation of books and writings so they could be shared with different cultures along the Silk Road.

---

[2] https://en.unesco.org/silkroad/content/did-you-know-silk-routes-mongols

He also sponsored scholars in their studies and education. Thanks to Kublai Khan, ancient knowledge that had been nearly lost was once again appreciated and preserved, and that information was spread alongside trade on the Silk Road. Records show over twenty thousand public schools were put in place during his time as emperor, which helped elevate the people of the region to become a better educated society.[3]

Another well-known person began his epic journey along the Silk Road during this same time period: Marco Polo.

Marco Polo served as a foreign emissary to Kublai Khan from 1215 to 1294, during which time he collected knowledge of the region, including Mongolian customs and inventions.

Although historians still debate whether Marco Polo ever traveled east, the writings about Marco Polo's journeys to the Far East introduced Europeans to the magic and wonder of lands they had never really imagined before. This fascination fueled the West to have more interest in trade with the East.

An illustration of Marco Polo's caravan to the East.

[3] https://courses.lumenlearning.com/suny-hccc-worldcivilization/chapter/kublai-khan/

14th to 15th Centuries CE

The times changed quickly during the period between the 14th and 15th centuries. The great Mongol Empire began to wane, with regional states developing in its place. These regional states were powerful. They blocked parts of the Silk Road, hindering the flow of goods and making travel more dangerous.

History produced another familiar name during this time, a very famous traveler along the Silk Road: the Black Death.

Due to the incubation period of the plague, the Silk Road was able to assist in the spread of the Black Death, as well as cultural exchange and exotic goods. People would pick up the illness in one area but not show any symptoms. Then, when they arrived at their next stop, they would fall ill and share their germs along a new area of the trade route. As you may imagine, the resulting panic and death caused trade to slow.

In addition to the Black Death, the fall of Constantinople during this same time period also contributed to the slowdown in trade along the Silk Road. Constantinople was the capital of the Byzantine Empire. The city connected the Eastern and Western trade routes, making it a vital hub for travelers looking to trade goods along both land and sea routes.

In 1453, the city was conquered by the Ottoman Turks, immediately causing a change in the flow of trade items due to new taxes and potential restrictions on goods that were allowed to be transported through the region. Constantinople was still a vibrant economic center under the Ottoman Empire; however, the higher tax rate was a major deterrent to the Silk Road trade. Trade links were severed, with the Ottoman Empire becoming the new middleman for trade with the East. This change in power caused a loss in stability for regular traders who were used to Byzantine-controlled Constantinople.[4]

The Age of Exploration was just beginning in Europe, and it was partially spurred on by the need to find a new trade route that did not include the fallen Constantinople. This led to the discovery of a maritime route that went around the tip of Africa, making long and cumbersome journeys over treacherous terrain a thing of the past for many eager tradesmen and further contributing to the decline of the Silk Road's land-based trade routes.

---

[4] https://www.tutorchase.com/answers/ib/history/what-economic-impacts-followed-the-fall-of-constantinople

16th to 18th Centuries CE

Welcome to the Age of Exploration! During this time, brave explorers sailed the ocean blue in search of shortcuts and new maritime trade routes to connect the East and the West.

Of course, you have likely heard of Christopher Columbus, but have you ever read about the Portuguese explorer Vasco da Gama? He sailed around the southernmost tip of Africa, Cape Hope, and reached the continent of India. This was a significant development in the world of trade. Europeans had traveled to India in boats for the first time, completely skipping over the land-based Silk Road trade paths.

Let us not forget to mention the Ottoman Empire. During the 16th to the 18th century, it was in control of important areas along the Silk Road, including the aforementioned city of Constantinople.

The Ottoman Empire also controlled Anatolia, a region that contained multiple trade routes, connecting the Ottoman Empire to central Asia, the Middle East, and Europe. The Ottomans actually controlled a very large swath of territory that included vital cities like Damascus, Aleppo, Baghdad, Beirut, and Jerusalem. They also held power over territories in North Africa, which was not a part of the overland trade routes but held important ports for maritime trade.

19th Century CE

The Silk Road became obsolete at this point in history. Colonies were the new popular thing for countries to establish, which meant ships were sailing all around the world. Instead of meandering along a treacherous landscape, people were now sailing directly to their trade destination, cutting out the need for a middleman and, along with it, ending the need for the ancient network of Silk Road pathways.

Now that you have gotten a broad overview of the Silk Road's timeline throughout history, let us take a deep dive into the factors that went behind the birth of the Silk Road. How did people trade before the Silk Road? Why did China wish to establish trade with the West?

Hop on your camel or a Tibetan horse if you prefer, and take a ride as we go way back to the Steppe Route and the Tea Horse Road.

Chapter 2: The Origins of the Silk Road

The Steppe Route

The very beginnings of trade pathways in China can be attributed to two routes: the Steppe Route and the Tea Horse Road.

The Steppe Route was an ancient trade route linking China with the Middle East, central Asia, and eventually the Mediterranean region.

Where exactly was the Steppe Route, though? Today, the route is occupied by the countries of Kazakhstan, northern Mongolia, the southern regions of Russia along the Caspian Sea and the Volga River, the southern parts of Ukraine, the Crimean Peninsula, areas of Turkmenistan along the Caspian Sea, and Uzbekistan.

The terrain was flat, open grassland in central Asia and eastern Europe. The soil and climate were not suitable for growing crops, but grass grew there in abundance. This grassy area went on for many miles and was home to nomadic tribes herding livestock. The flat terrain made travel easy for tradesmen traveling in caravans of horses and camels.

The Eurasian Steppe Route was dissected by rougher areas, such as the Ural Mountains, the Altai Mountains, the Sayan Mountains, and the Greater Khingan range.

When looking at our timeline for the Silk Road, we have to consider where to place the beginnings of the Steppe Route. It was around long before the Silk Road became established in history; in fact, it was around before our timeline even began.

The Steppe Route has no formal beginning. It started in antiquity, as far back as humans have been living in central Asia. Scholars estimate the Steppe Route began in the 4th millennium BCE, possibly around the Bronze Age.

It is important to note a world-altering invention that showed up in central Asia during the Bronze Age: the spoked wheel. Wheeled transport undoubtedly played a role in the beginnings of long-distance trade. As wagons and chariots were developed, people discovered they could move goods over longer distances. With those goods, people came into contact with different cultures, and the sharing of ideas began.

The Steppe Route grew alongside the rise of Inner Eurasian pastoralism.[5] These would be the first farmers of the Steppe, the people who practiced animal husbandry. Unsurprisingly, the first trade routes followed the paths made by nomadic livestock herders.

Initially, nomadic people were hesitant to travel and trade. As their groups grew larger, more resources were needed, fueling the need to explore further. As people explored, they came into contact with different tribes and cultures. Theft became an issue, which prompted nomads to build fences for their livestock and design defenses for their tribes. People banded together in cultural communities to support each other.

As weather patterns changed, the nomads were forced to move from place to place to find better grazing land. This was a key factor in the early development of trade routes. Nomads were forced to come into contact with each other whether they liked it or not.

Soon, trade between civilizations and nomadic tribes became frequent along the Steppe Route as people shared goods between cultures. Few people traveled the full length of the trade route, though. Instead, middlemen and intermediaries were used to pass goods throughout the region of central Asia and into the Middle East (they would be similar to couriers).

Scholars estimate that the Steppe Route was in use at least two thousand years prior to the Silk Road.[6]

---

[5] Christian, David. "Silk Roads or Steppe Roads?" https://www.jstor.org/stable/20078816.
[6] Torr, Geordie. *The Silk Roads: A History of the Great Trading Routes Between East and West.*

As the years passed, the route gradually expanded until it reached the Mediterranean Sea. The original Steppe Route is now known as the Northern Silk Road.

Travelers along the route exchanged silk and other textiles. Gemstones, such as turquoise, lapis lazuli, agate, and nephrite, were just some of the riches exchanged between regions. Ceramics, spices, and precious metals were exchanged too.

Travel contributed to the spread of Buddhism from India into central Asia and China. Politically, the riches made from trade helped to grow the powerful Persian Empire, the Parthian Empire, and eventually the Islamic caliphates.

The Steppe Route was the main artery that formed the blueprint for the Silk Road and set the stage for what would become the most historically significant trade route in history. Early political diplomacy and the new linguistic connections that formed over time were essential elements that helped form the future of the Silk Road.

The Tea Horse Road

The Tea Horse Road was another early artery of the Silk Road. Ancient Chinese records refer to *Chamadao*, which translates to "the tea and horse road."

The Tea Horse Road was precisely what its name described. That is to say, it was a road primarily established for the trade of two things: Chinese tea leaves and Tibetan horses.

The Chinese in the 1st century CE were a military society. Horses were exceedingly valuable for moving men from place to place and for riding into battle. Horses also played an essential role in moving people and goods along dangerous and tedious trade routes.

Imagine the ultimate battle horse, one with all of the most powerful features: extreme endurance, surefootedness over rocky mountainous terrain, a body unfazed by the high altitudes of the region, fur and skin that could withstand wild winds and biting snow, and the physical strength to survive off of very little food in remote areas without access to grazing pastures. Basically, this super horse could eat three blades of grass and charge fearlessly into a wintery battle scene on a rocky slope.

For other people, instead of charging into battle, this super horse would fearlessly navigate along narrow pathways and through harsh weather along trade routes.

The Chinese were in luck because neighboring Tibet just so happened to breed horses that met this exact description.

The rough terrain of Himalayan Tibet was a unique environment to breed horses. As a result of the high altitude and rocky slopes, Tibetan horses evolved to become perfect creatures for perilous trade routes. They could make it over mountains and through blizzards and the shifting sands of the desert.

A Tibetan horse was also associated with a high social status, similar to the fast foreign sports cars of today. This made them a hot trade item.

You may laugh when you think of the Chinese offering to trade some tea leaves for a powerful, well-bred horse. The Tibetans, however? They were not laughing. They were pleased to make the trade.

The importance of tea leaves was paramount in Chinese and Tibetan societies. They provided medicinal benefits. Tea was associated with hospitality, friendship, and gatherings, especially along the Silk Road. Sophisticated families could offer tea to Silk Road travelers. Tea provided an assuage for the senses with its smell, taste, and even rich colors. In some areas, tea leaves could even be used as currency.[7]

Not every region along the Silk Road could grow tea due to the harsh climates, which further upped the allure of tea leaves as a trade item.

And for the Chinese? Tea leaves were lightweight and easy to transport. They took up little space when stored in bricks that weighed between 0.45 kilograms and 2.75 kilograms.[8] The tea leaves also sold at a high price.

The Chinese and Tibetans began traveling up and down the Tea Horse Road between China and Tibet, establishing an essential trade route that would later become known as the Southern Silk Road or the Southwest Silk Road. This road was one of the most prominent parts of the webbed pathways making up the Silk Road.

The Han Dynasty

Perhaps the most important early contributor to the Silk Road was the Han dynasty (206 BCE–220 CE). The Han dynasty decided to start formally making trade agreements with the areas around them and then

---

[7] "Ancient Tea and Horse Caravan Road."
http://www.silkroadfoundation.org/newsletter/2004vol2num1/tea.htm.

[8] "Ancient Tea Horse Road." https://www.bbc.com/travel/article/20120830-asias-ancient-tea-horse-road.

with regions that were farther away.

In 138 BCE, Emperor Wu Di of the Han dynasty decided he wanted to send a court official to make contact with the Yuezhi, one of their traditional allies. The emperor learned that the Yuezhi were being threatened by the Han dynasty's common enemy, the Xiongnu.

To reach the Yuezhi, whoever volunteered to go would need to pass west through territory controlled by the Xiongnu. Only one person was brave enough to take the journey: a petty court official named Zhang Qian.

He set out with a party of one hundred men. Unluckily for Zhang Qian, he was captured by the Xiongnu. They held him captive for ten years, forcing him to move with the imperial party as they traveled around the Steppe. During that time, he married a Xiongnu woman and had several children.

Zhang Qian made his way to the Yuezhi kingdom but was unsuccessful in making a treaty with them. He stayed for a year before attempting the journey home to report back to the emperor.

Zhang Qian was captured by the Xiongnu a second time, but he managed to escape with his wife and children during a disturbance in the Xiongnu camp. Zhang Qian was away for thirteen years in total.

Upon his release, he continued traveling around central Asia, where he explored the wealthy civilizations that had flourished under Alexander the Great. These Hellenistic Greek cities had arts and culture that Zhang had never seen before. He reported back to the emperor that the cities were heavily fortified with walls, towers, and gates. He also told the emperor about all the wonders he had witnessed, which unfortunately were not recorded in detail for us to read in the present day.

We can guess what he saw from what we know about Hellenistic cities, though. The cities were laid out in grids using organized urban planning. They featured public buildings like libraries, gyms, and bathhouses. They were famous for their theaters, amphitheaters, and stone walkways.

Most importantly, Zhang Qian visited markets in each city, where he saw goods that he had never seen before.

The emperor was intrigued, so he sent Zhang Qian back out on the road to explore further. Thankfully, the diplomat was not held prisoner on this trip. Instead, he made his way to Persia, where he discovered a new breed of horses in what is present-day Uzbekistan. These were known as the Ferghana horse, and they were said to be so powerful that they sweat blood.

Scientists have now made an educated guess that the bloody sweat was likely drops of blood from biting parasites. A little less impressive, on the whole, but in ancient times, it seemed pretty amazing. The people believed these powerful horses were the result of interbreeding mortal and heavenly horses.

Emperor Wudi wanted to hear more about the horses. He even wanted some for himself. Zhang Qian also told him of amazing glassware and of a new type of bamboo he had never seen before. There was also an unusual cloth they were selling, which was reported to have come from India, a place completely unknown to the Han dynasty.

Zhang Qian is now historically known as the "Father of the Silk Road," which seems like a title he certainly earned with his determination and perseverance.

The biggest question we might be asking about the Han dynasty is why. Why did the emperor decide to pursue trade outside of his local region?

Curiosity about unknown places like India and new exotic goods was definitely a strong motivator. But was that enough inspiration to send more men out on perilous journeys? Remember, this was a period fraught with warring tribes and unfriendly civilizations. The only way to establish diplomatic relationships with other people groups and cultures was to ride up on a horse and say hello, which could be somewhat risky if the diplomat was not a welcome visitor. (See Zhang Qian's experiences and failed treaty attempt!)

Yet, the Han dynasty still pursued the idea of establishing trade far from home. What were its other reasons beyond curiosity?

The Han dynasty's first reason was a selfish one. If the Han dynasty wanted to expand beyond its borders, it could either start a battle and claim territory or gradually spread its influence through diplomacy and trade with neighboring states. Instead of choosing violence, the Han dynasty chose to be peaceful. It formed treaties with its neighbors to prevent any conflicts and established solid trade agreements that were mutually beneficial for both parties.

The Han dynasty intelligently used trade to foster alliances, which allowed it a buffer from contentious relationships with other regions, especially the Xiongnu Confederation to its north. These alliances made the empire more secure and far less vulnerable to sudden attacks or takeovers. The Han dynasty now had friends in its corner, ready to stand together if needed because everyone was benefiting from the trade of goods and the sharing of ideas.

Sneakily, the Han dynasty also began to establish something known as protectorates. Of course, if trade routes were to be established, they had to be safe and secure, right?

When the trade routes extended outside of the Han dynasty's region and snaked through dangerous territory, someone had to be in charge to keep the peace and safety of the tradesmen. How were they going to protect the traded goods from theft?

While setting up these protected routes, the Han dynasty had the opportunity to exert its influence over the government in these regions, further expanding its power by sticking its fingers in its neighbor's governments.

As the officially established trade routes grew, the Han dynasty began to reap the economic benefits of reliable, organized trade. The emperor decided to invest in the military. The Han traded for powerful Ferghana horses and grew their cavalry. They fought off the nomads and began building their own fortified walls, which would later be part of the Great Wall of China.

The wall served as a defense, naturally, but it had another use. Travelers were forced to pay a tax to the emperor on the goods they were carrying. This added to the wealth of the Han dynasty. There were only a few gates in the Great Wall for travelers to pass through. These quickly became centers of trade along the Silk Road. Soon, there were inns for weary travelers, markets to trade goods, and restaurants. These ports of entry also began to serve as border patrol and customs locations for the empire.

Next, the Han dynasty invested in its own administration, growing its government. The Han started making scientific advancements, too! It is amazing what a steady cash flow can do. Suddenly, the Han dynasty was measuring time with water clocks and inventing paper to write on. Paper exploded in popularity and eventually became a heavily traded item along the Silk Road.

Paper was especially important to the spread of Buddhism. Scripture was written down and easily transported along the earliest routes of the Silk Road. Paper allowed scripture and teachings to be translated into various languages and dialects and to be saved for academic study.

Buddhism spread like wildfire with the support of Chinese leaders, but we will talk more about that later.

While physical goods were being traded, something even more powerful was happening intangibly. The Han dynasty was asserting what is known as soft power over those it interacted with on the trade route.

Soft power refers to the influence of a nation over other people. The Han dynasty was sharing its values, ideas, philosophies, and culture without using force. It was happening naturally as people from the Han dynasty interacted with others along the trade route. By sharing their music, art, fashion, and food, they were able to create a sense of unity between different cultures, strengthening their alliances and securing their position on the world trade stage.

The foundations for the Silk Road were officially laid in place by the diplomatic pursuits of the Han dynasty. A physical road was not built, but the network of treaties, alliances, and protectorates created by the Han dynasty set the stage for the east-to-west sharing of both goods and cultures to take off and explode into a superhighway. Wealthy empires waited at either end of the Silk Road, clamoring for luxury items from the opposite end of the trade route.

The emergence of the Silk Road is still a topic of study among anthropologists, archaeologists, and historians today. Archaeological discoveries at the Eurasian Steppe along the Steppe Route have forced historians to rethink what they thought they knew about life in the 2nd century BCE. Gravesites and tombs reveal grave goods that are from a different culture than the deceased, proving that trade was booming earlier than previously thought.

DNA testing and grave detecting from satellites are two of the modern tools now available to archaeologists that have put a new spin on the emergence of the Silk Road. The story is still changing as we learn new facts with each excavation.

Chapter 3: The Great Empires of the Silk Road

Arguably, one of the most fascinating things about looking back at history with clear hindsight is the ability to view the rise and fall of empires across the globe. The Silk Road is particularly fascinating in that it served as a thread to knit together empires and clearly contributed to both the rise and, at times, the fall of great and powerful empires.

The four main empires that thrived along the Silk Road were the Persian Empire, the Hellenistic Parthian Empire, the Roman Empire, and the Tang dynasty.

The Persian Empire (550 BCE–330 BCE)

The Persian Empire at its greatest extent in 500 BCE.

Cattette, CC BY 4.0 <https://creativecommons.org/licenses/by/4.0>, via Wikimedia Commons; https://commons.wikimedia.org/wiki/File:Achaemenid_Empire_500_BCE.jpg

You may have heard of the famous Persian Empire referenced in history and stories. Even if you are not familiar with the details, chances are you know of some of Persia's most famous wares. For example, have you ever seen a Persian rug?

The Persian Empire was also known as the Achaemenid Empire. It was famous for rock carvings and metalwork, among many other things. It was also the first civilization to develop a postal service using its Royal Road.

The Persian Empire stretched from regions of Iran to Iraq, across Egypt and Turkey, and into central Asia. The central location of Persia gave the empire control over essential parts of the earliest predecessor to the Silk Road: the Royal Road. The Persian Empire's famous Royal Road was an ancient highway that ran from the eastern city of Susa to the western city of Sardis, crossing most of the Persian Empire. The Royal Road would become an integral piece of the trade route and laid a major part of the foundation for the larger Silk Road network.

Unlike the Silk Road's treacherous web of trade route paths, the Royal Road was designed for ease of travel. Its purpose was quick communication and efficient transportation from city to city. The Royal Road had multiple relay stations, where couriers waited to carry messages from one point to the next, making communication across the empire a speedy affair in the days before emails or text messages. The Royal Road also provided the administration with a way to communicate effectively across many miles. The Royal Road allowed the Persian army to march quickly across all sections of the large empire, keeping Persia strong and secure.

The Silk Road was never intended to move men and messages across a vast empire like the Royal Road. However, as time went on, the trade routes became more consolidated under the Mongol Empire. It was at this time the Silk Road intersected with the Royal Road at multiple points, adding another layer of depth to the strength and vitality of the Silk Road trade network and making the historical Royal Road one of the most important channels of the Silk Road.

Susa, in today's modern Iran, was possibly the most important city on the intersecting routes. Due to its geographical location, Susa was one of the key points between the East and the West. Goods traded there included textiles, silks, dyes, spices, dried fruits, nuts, grains, herbs, precious metals, metalwork such as tools, magnificent gemstones, pottery, ceramics, paper, books, and manuscripts with knowledge of other cultures and religions.

Another important city along the two routes was Ctesiphon. This city is now modern-day Baghdad, Iraq. The Tigris River runs through this region. Ctesiphon was known for both the trade of goods and diplomatic interactions between cities, states, and empires since so many travelers passed through the area.

Persepolis was the capital of the Persian Empire. It was not directly linked to the Silk Road, but it was a main stop along the Royal Road, as it was the empire's hub of political administration and power. It is worth mentioning this city since it played such a vital role in trade and diplomatic interactions along the route.

The Royal Road ended in Sardis, which is in modern-day Turkey. After Sardis, the Silk Road continued to connect to other regions through maritime trade routes across the Mediterranean Sea, making Sardis a key location for cultural exchange.

There is one intangible thing that the Persian Empire used its Silk Road connections to spread. It was a religion, but it was not the Islamic religion that has become almost synonymous with the Middle East today.

The Persian Empire's religion was called Zoroastrianism. This was a monotheistic religion, meaning they believed in a single god. It was named after the Persian prophet Zoroaster, also known as Zarathustra. Zoroaster broke out of the typical belief systems held by other Indo-Iranian groups who worshiped multiple deities. Thanks in part to the Silk Road, his monotheistic belief system began to spread like wildfire. Many scholars agree that Zoroastrianism is the world's first monotheistic faith.

What is the name of Zoroastrianism's single god? It is Ahura Mazda, at least according to a vision Zoroaster had when he was thirty years old. Its temples were known as fire temples, places of worship containing an altar and an eternal flame.

You may now be asking what Zoroastrianism has to do with the Silk Road.

Well, as mentioned, Zoroaster's messages spread along the Silk Road with traded goods. It is possible that the tenets of Zoroastrianism helped influence bits and pieces of the three major Abrahamic religions: Judaism, Christianity, and Islam.

For example, word about Zoroastrianism reached the Kingdom of Judea, where the Jewish people were living in captivity. The major ideas of Zoroastrianism are a single god, heaven, hell, and a day of judgment. Does this sound familiar to anyone else?

Imagine for just a moment the impact Abrahamic religions have had on the world throughout history.

As Zoroastrianism spread along the Silk Road, it laid the foundation for the basis of religions that would contribute to many things, both positive and negative. Countless famous works of art have been based on monotheistic religions. How many institutions of higher learning have been based on these religions? In the Middle Ages, the religious medieval European, Middle Eastern, and African universities played a crucial role in spreading knowledge far and wide.

Common morals were established between cultures and countries, with a monotheistic religion as the common denominator. These morals contributed to the basis of laws and constitutions used by governments across the world. Colonies were created, wars were waged, and people groups were oppressed and conquered all in the name of a monotheistic religion.

Without Zoroastrianism spreading along the Silk Road, the worldview for many countries and cultures throughout history and even today would likely look very different.

Eventually, the great Persian Empire outgrew its britches. The empire expanded along the eastern shore of the Mediterranean, and the Persians thought they could add Greek colonies to the empire. However, this backfired somewhat since the colonies, which were located along the edge of modern-day Turkey, were not very excited to become Persian.

When the Greek colonies rebelled, they were given support by mainland Greek city-states, effectively starting a war between Persia and Greece that would ultimately end in the downfall of the Persian Empire.

The Parthian Empire (247 BCE–224 CE)

As the Persian Empire declined, the next great civilization to rise up on the timeline of history was the Parthian Empire.

You may be familiar with the famous Hellenistic period. This period occurred alongside the Parthian Empire on our timeline. The Parthian Empire was located farther to the east, where it took in some Hellenistic influences from neighbors traveling along the Silk Road.

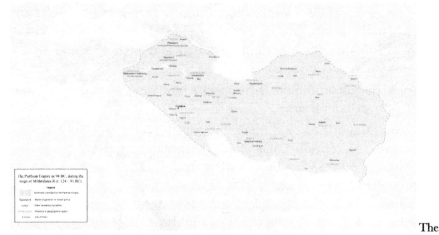

The

Parthian Empire at its greatest extent in 94 BCE.

Original file by Ro4444, edited by me, CC BY-SA 4.0 <https://creativecommons.org/licenses/by-sa/4.0>, via Wikimedia Commons

https://commons.wikimedia.org/wiki/File:Map_of_the_Parthian_Empire_under_Mithridates_II.svg

The heart of the Parthian Empire was located in modern-day Iran. To the east, the empire covered what is today parts of Turkey, Armenia, and Turkmenistan. The empire spread outward from Iran north to the Caspian Sea. In the south, it went all the way to the Persian Gulf. Like many empires, the borders of the Parthian Empire changed throughout its history.

The position of the Parthian Empire along the Silk Road allowed the empire to control overland trade between the Mediterranean and Asia. The capture of key cities on the Persian Gulf gave the Parthian Empire control over vital commercial centers for maritime trade.

As a power play, the Parthians used their mighty military and their geographical position to gatekeep the silk trade. They refused to allow the Romans to trade directly with the Chinese Han dynasty, which had the coveted silk. The Parthians kept themselves planted firmly in the center as middlemen between the Han and Rome.

The *Hou Hanshu* (*Book of the Later Han*) is a well-known historical account of the Han dynasty written by Fan Ye, who lived from 398 to 445 CE. This quote from the *Hou Hanshu* explains what the Han discovered about Parthia's gatekeeping of the silk trade along the Silk Road.

"They [the Romans] trade with Anxi [Parthia] and Tianzhu [Northwest India] by sea. The profit margin is ten to one. The king of this country always wanted to send envoys to Han, but Anxi, wishing to control the trade in multi-colored Chinese silks, blocked the route to prevent [the Romans] getting through [to China]."[9]

The government of the Parthian Empire recognized how important Parthia's position was as intermediaries on the Silk Road. The politicians enjoyed the wealth, and in turn, they prioritized a strong army and an organized state to keep everything along their part of the Silk Road running smoothly without conflict.

The importance of trade was so well recognized that, despite tensions, conflicts between the Han dynasty, the Roman Empire, and the Parthians were resolved peacefully. During this time period, the Roman emperor sent a letter to the Parthian ruler asking that they form an alliance with each other based on their trade of spices and textiles. The deal was successfully agreed upon.

Diplomacy was the goal of all three empires. The development of positive relations between empires through the tenets of diplomacy was just another world-changing tally mark on the list of concepts heavily influenced by the existence of the Silk Road. People realized the mutual success of economies through commercial trade, even between countries and empires that had tensions with each other, was more important than fighting.

The Roman Republic (509-27 BCE) and The Roman Empire (27 BCE-476 CE)

Unlike other empires we have discussed, the Roman Republic and the Roman Empire did not directly use the Silk Road as a main trade route. The Roman use of the Silk Road was rather indirect, going through intermediaries like the Parthians to make contact with the Far East.

In the year 53 BCE, the Romans suffered what is known as one of their worst military defeats. Marcus Licinius Crassus and his men were defeated by the Parthian Empire at the Battle of Carrhae.

The battle raged throughout the morning hours, with waves of Parthian men attacking the Roman troops repeatedly. The Romans held strong and did not waver, hoping they would still be able to defeat the Parthians and win the battle.

---

[9] Fan Ye. *Hou Hanshu* (*Book of the Later Han*).

It was just after noon when something completely unexpected occurred. The Parthians staged another round of attacks, this time with a twist. The Parthian soldiers came running into battle, banging on drums, shooting arrows, and making a cacophony of noise. As the Roman soldiers looked on in shock, the Parthians unfurled bright, shimmering silk banners.

Roman Historian Lucius Annaeus Florus, who lived from 74 to 130 CE, gives a description of the silk banners.

"And so he [Crassus] had scarcely reached Carrhae when the king's generals, Silaces and Surenus, displayed all around him their standards, uttering with gold and silken pennons; then without delay the cavalry, pouring around on all sides, showered their weapons as thick as hail or rain upon them. Thus, the army was destroyed in lamentable slaughter."[10]

No one is certain if the silk banners were opened to rally the Parthian troops or if the Parthians actually meant to shock the Romans, but in any case, the Romans stood with their mouths agape.

They had never before seen silk. The bold colors, the brilliant way the material reflected the light on the battlefield, and the beauty of the textile stunned them. This moment's pause allowed the Parthians to gain the foothold they needed. The Roman soldiers began running in shock and breaking rank, giving the Parthians the advantage in battle.

Of course, the entire battle was not lost simply because the Romans saw the dazzling banners. Other factors were at play, namely some poor battle strategy decisions made by Crassus and the excellent military strategies used by the Parthians.

Some historians believe this fateful day was the first time the Roman Empire came in contact with silk. From then on, the Romans wanted to find a way to get silk for themselves. The door was opened to begin trading along the Silk Road to acquire this luxurious textile from the Chinese. Soon, the Roman elite were clamoring to get their hands on as much expensive silk as they could.

For the Romans, silk was a mysterious textile. They had no knowledge of the silkworms the Chinese bred and used to create the beautiful cloth. Some thought it grew on trees. Others were suspicious that the love of silk

---

[10] https://archive.org/stream/in.crnet.dli.2015.184585/2015.184585.Lucius-Annaeus-Florus_djvu.txt pg. 212.

would cause jealousy and immorality and make men want to own an excess of goods that would leave the empire weakened by selfishness.

The Roman obsession with silk did not die down. Instead, it grew into a mania until the Romans were trading silk and other luxury items through intermediaries as quickly as they could. Silk was incredibly expensive, comparable to pearls or purple dye, and was often striped with gold, further driving up the wow factor and the cost.

During the first two centuries of the Common Era, the Romans imported various other luxury goods alongside the silk threads. They purchased precious stones, such as pearls and emeralds, and spices. Indian and Arabic spices like nutmeg, cloves, cardamom, and pepper were some of the most popular spices that had double uses. Spices were not just for eating—they also served as aphrodisiacs to go along with the allure of the sensual silks.

Historians estimate the Romans were spending the present-day equivalent of up to one billion dollars USD on luxury imports per year by 65 CE!

In the 4th century CE, the Roman Empire promoted the tolerance of Christianity under Emperor Constantine, which led to many people converting to Christianity. Cities along trade routes suddenly became hubs of the religion. This had a lasting impact on the spread of Christianity along the Silk Road.

Missionaries also went out along the Silk Road to establish churches in the biggest trade and port cities. They used the tradesmen and intermediaries to spread the seeds of Christianity from west to east.

Throughout the long history of the Silk Road, the Romans and the Chinese both gained immense amounts of soft power through trade. They spread their cultural influences far and wide. The Chinese grew rich from the trade of silk, and the Romans gained economic benefits from sending their own goods to the Chinese, which included wine and brightly colored glass vases that became a prized luxury good in China.

A green Roman glass cup found in an Eastern Han tomb.

However, with all the mutual benefits the two empires shared, they did not meet face to face, only exchanging goods through many hands along the route between China and the Mediterranean.

How would history have been different if the Chinese and the Romans directly interacted with each other? We can guess, but we will never truly know the answer.

The Tang Dynasty (618–907 CE)

There is one major empire involved in the Silk Road trade that we have not yet mentioned: the Tang dynasty in China.

To give a clear picture of our timeline, the Tang dynasty existed alongside the rise of medieval European states and the beginning of the Middle Ages. India was also beginning its medieval period. In the Americas, the Maya civilization was collapsing, and the Post-Classic period was beginning. The Byzantine Empire and the Islamic caliphates were in conflict and also involved in trade along the Silk Road.

The world was becoming a busy place. As people began to explore more, trade and diplomacy were of the utmost importance on the world stage. The rulers of the Tang dynasty recognized the importance of trade for their empire. Infrastructure was very important to keep trade moving along smoothly throughout the region.

The Tang dynasty prided itself on organization and administration. They had around 32,100 kilometers (19,900 miles) of postal routes throughout the region, with mail carried by both horse and boat.[11]

The Tang dynasty preferred to move a large amount of goods within China by boat. The Chinese built their famous Grand Canal during the Sui dynasty (581–618 CE). During the Tang dynasty, the canal was expanded and meticulously maintained. The canal moved goods between the Yellow River and the Yangtze River, including grain that was taken as payment for taxes, agricultural products, and the military. The Grand Canal connected northern and southern China by boat.

The military transports along the canal allowed China to maintain a strong, secure country. Threats could be quickly extinguished, with troops and horses, along with their artillery, speeding down the canal at a moment's notice. Similar to the Silk Road, knowledge, culture, and ideas also traveled with the men who sailed down the canal and back. This helped China unify as a country, as the north and the south began sharing common ideals.

The Tang dynasty quickly took advantage of this efficient transportation route. They began charging a tax for merchants to transport goods along the Grand Canal, boosting its economy.

The Silk Road intersected with the Grand Canal at various port cities, which became multicultural hubs of trade. Yangzhou, Suzhou, and Hangzhou were a few of these hub cities. Merchants from the Silk Road gathered in these cities to trade goods.

One hub of international trade that is still famous in China today is the Tang West Market in Xi'an (then known as Chang'an).

Chang'an was an important city during the Tang dynasty that hosted the largest market in the world during that time period. Archaeological surveys show the market was about one square kilometer or 0.4 square miles. The market was divided into nine rectangular regions, similar to city blocks, with more than two hundred types of goods being traded in thousands of different stores. An estimated 150,000 people a day came through the market.

---

[11] "Trade under the Tang Dynasty." https://courses.lumenlearning.com/suny-hccc-worldcivilization/chapter/trade-under-the-tang-dynasty/.

The sellers were both local and international, with the goods heavily influenced by trade on the Silk Road. Chang'an became a center of cultural studies for people along the Silk Road, thanks to being a hub of trade and all of the friendly political diplomacy surrounding the Tang West Market. Many scholars from other regions longed to come to Chang'an to study.

The Silk Road and the Grand Canal were both instrumental in creating the Tang West Market and catapulting Chang'an into such a unique, multicultural municipality.

You have certainly heard of the famous Panama Canal. You may be surprised to learn that the Tang dynasty's Grand Canal is twenty-two times longer than the Panama Canal. The Panama Canal is only around fifty miles (eighty kilometers) in length. China's Grand Canal is 1,104 miles (1,776 kilometers) long! It was quite an engineering feat for the time period during which it was constructed.

The Grand Canal was constructed over a period of six years in order to connect the capital city of Beijing to the city of Hangzhou in the southern farming region of China. The Grand Canal was not an entirely new canal; rather, it was a project made to connect multiple existing canals across China.

For example, there was already a canal between the Yangtze River and the Huai River and another canal called the Hong Gou Canal that connected the Yellow River to the Bian River. These ancient canals grew into the Grand Canal under the strict leadership of Emperor Yang during the Sui dynasty, a short-lived dynasty that preceded the Tang dynasty.

Emperor Yang was known for his tyrannical ways, forcing many farmers to work themselves to death on the Grand Canal project. Although the exact number is not known, it took millions of Chinese men to construct the canal. The project was finally completed in 609 CE.

By the 1400s, the Grand Canal was bustling with activity. The Chinese government had over eleven thousand barges in use for transporting grain up and down the canal. During that period, there were more than forty-five thousand workers who maintained the canal on a regular basis.

While the citizens were busy constructing the Grand Canal and trading goods during the Tang dynasty, the administration was feverishly bustling around the Silk Road on many diplomatic missions. In fact, the Tang dynasty made friendly contact with more than three hundred different regions along the trade routes.[12]

The Tang dynasty presented a united China, drawing together smaller tribes and different regions with a more unified culture. The Tang dynasty was partly aided by the spread of information along the Grand Canal, resulting in strong national power. Ambassadors from the Tang dynasty were curious people and very adept at understanding new cultures or making intelligent assessments of new places. This gave these passionate ambassadors an advantage on the world stage, making them wildly successful and prosperous at peaceful trade along the Silk Road.

---

[12] "The Prosperity of the Silk Road in the Tang Dynasty."
http://en.shaanxi.gov.cn/as/hac/hos/201704/t20170428_1595517.html.

Chapter 4: The Silk Road's Most Valuable Goods

Now that we know the major role played by the Silk Road in world history, perhaps we should discuss what was traded along the Silk Road. Of course, silk was the most famous item; after all, the route was named after it. While silk undoubtedly left an indescribable mark on world history, it was not the only important thing shared between countries and cultures along the Silk Road.

Silk

As legend has it, around the year 3000 BCE, Empress Leizu was having a cup of tea when a silkworm cocoon plopped down from the tree above right into her cup. Surprised, the empress pulled the cocoon out of her tea and began to unroll it. She admired the long, silky fibers and decided to try weaving some of them.

The result was magnificent. Her husband, the Yellow Emperor, recommended she study the life of the silkworm. She instructed her servants to help her begin cultivating silkworms, and it was then that Empress Leizu became famous in Chinese mythology as the goddess of silk.

This story is just a legend passed down through the generations. What has history actually uncovered about the beginnings of silk? Since silk is a delicate textile, it does not survive well in tombs or graves, but archaeologists have still been able to uncover quite a few clues about the origins of silk in human history.

More than 8,500 years ago, humanity was in the Neolithic Age or, as some prefer to call it, the New Stone Age. Humans had recently transitioned from hunting and gathering to cultivating crops and breeding livestock. They also created settled agricultural communities, which became the first villages. People had more time with their settled lifestyles, so they began to experiment with metalworking, spend more time on religion, and develop their artistic talents.

Pottery was a common art form during this period. Almost every artistic creation had a practical use. Bowls or jugs were decorated with scenes depicting daily life, religion, or intricate patterns but were used for cooking or storage.

Surprisingly, silk weaving was possibly one of the first arts practiced in Neolithic China. Archaeologists discovered the remnants of silk fibroin inside Neolithic tombs that were excavated in Jiahu, China.

While the exact date has not been pinpointed, these tombs were from the period between 7000 and 5000 BCE. Alongside the silk fibers, archaeologists discovered remnants of bone needles and weaving tools.

In nearby Shanxi, pieces of a cleanly cut silk cocoon were discovered while excavating a site left behind by the Yangshao culture. This suggests that between 4000 and 3000 BCE, humans were breeding silkworms. A solid white cocoon only comes from the domesticated silkworm.

At a Yangshao excavation site dated to 3630 BCE, a woven silk wrap was discovered shrouding the body of a child placed inside a burial urn. This is the earliest sample archaeologists have found of intact silk woven textiles.

For many years, China had a ban on the import of silkworms. Silkworm cultivation, or sericulture, was a closely guarded Chinese secret. It was so secretive that other cultures who enjoyed the trade of this gorgeous textile along the Silk Road began developing their own origin stories to explain how silk was produced. The Romans, for example, were convinced that silk came from special tree leaves.

Did you know that in China, sericulture and silk weaving was only for the richest in society? It was an art form mainly for women, and at first, it was restricted to only the imperial family. As time went on, silk was also allowed for noble women. It was not until the Qing dynasty (1644-1911) that everyday peasants were allowed access to silk.

During the Han dynasty, which was the origins of the official Silk Road on our timeline, silk became far more than just a textile. Silk was similar to gold in that it was used as payments to the government alongside bronze coins. Silk was shared with other powers when Chinese emperors sent out diplomatic missions to explore and establish trade across neighboring regions.

Silk was also given as payment to soldiers, who then traded the silk with nomads, who then traded the silk with others. You can easily see how silk became one of the most prominent goods traded along the famous trade route from the Silk Road's earliest point in known history.

As outside cultures saw the beauty of shimmering silk, they became hooked. Silk skyrocketed in popularity among the elite and wealthy as one of the most popular luxury goods to ever exist on planet Earth.

Silk left a lasting impact on the global economy. It bridged cultures, bringing together regions that would have otherwise likely been at war with each other (not to say that silk was a magical item that prevented war, but it did make empires think twice before attacking since it would impact trade). It boosted economies and inspired trade all across Asia and Europe. Today, silk is still a luxury good, with China still producing around 80 percent of the world's silk.

Spices

Have you ever come face to face with the ferocious Cinnamologus?

It is very likely you have not because this fabled bird lived some 2,500 years ago. Arab traders told the ancient Greeks and Romans how they used chunks of meat to trick the Cinnamologus and lure it away from the nest. When the Cinnamologus grabbed the big pieces of meat and flew back to its nest, the weight of the bird landing with the meat caused the big nest to collapse, scattering sticks of cinnamon for the traders to collect.

The cassia spice has a similar origin story. The Greek historian Herodotus said that cassia was collected in a lake that was protected by "winged creatures like bats, which screeched alarmingly and were very pugnacious."[13]

The international trade of spices along the Silk Road was very closely guarded by tradesmen. They did not want to share their secret sources for the spices for fear of others edging in on their sources. Thus, the tall tales were born, and they were even believed by people who lived far away

---

[13] Herodotus. *Histories.*

from the Eastern spice-growing lands.

Fantastical origin stories spread across Europe during the Middle Ages as people tried to understand where their spices came from. One story that still exists today tells us that cloves were gathered by nets from the Nile River in Egypt. People in the West had no idea where these spices packed full of flavor originated from, and the tradesmen wanted to keep it that way to secure their business.

Today, we can purchase almost any sort of spice or seasoning at the grocery store, in a cultural market, or even online with ease. Years ago, before our world was interconnected with travel, people were limited to what plants grew in their own regions. As you can imagine, this led to very little culinary variety.

The value of spices and dried herbs was exceedingly high for traders. They had multiple uses; for instance, they could be used for flavoring or medicine. Best of all, they were very easy to transport. Spices took up little space, which was important when traveling by caravan or sailing on a small boat. The value to weight ratio of spices made them a lucrative trade item.

The word "spices" is derived from the Latin term *species*, which translates to "special wares." Spices were no ordinary trade item; they were a little different than ordinary trade items and often far more valuable.

While spices were traded along the traditional land routes of the Silk Road, the most efficient and well-known spice trading was done along the maritime Silk Road routes. These sea routes stretched from the west coast of Japan, circled around the islands of Indonesia, made stops in India and the Middle East, then crossed the Mediterranean Sea to arrive in Europe, where spices spread across the continent all the way into present-day Great Britain. Historians say the spice trade marked the beginning of globalization.

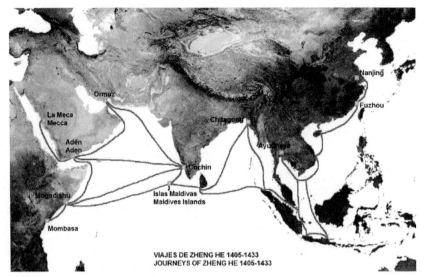

The maritime routes of the Silk Road. You can also see the routes taken by Zheng He, a Muslim admiral who explored Southeast Asia, the Middle East, and other regions in the 15th century.

What spices were traded along the Silk Road?

Most of the spices during the time of the Silk Road came from tropical plants that could only be grown in the heat and moisture of the Far East, not the cooler, dryer climates of Europe. In Europe, people could grow herbs like basil, mint, rosemary, and thyme, but the stronger spices came from the tropics, thousands of miles away, making them an exotic delicacy.

Among these spices were pepper, cloves, mace, and cumin. These spices were expensive, but affluent noblemen could afford them.

Pepper was transported in carefully guarded caravans because it was such a sought-after item. The Romans used pepper in their dishes in the 1st century CE. Peppercorns only grew along the coast of India and the Indonesian islands, so they could only reach Rome and Europe along the trade routes. Cloves, mace, and cumin were transported in the same manner as pepper. They were initially traded along maritime routes and then along the Silk Road in packs on the backs of camels or in wagons so they could be guarded from thieves.

The most valuable spices were worth more than their weight in gold. These spices were cinnamon, nutmeg, ginger, and saffron. These expensive spices were only available to the most elite people in society.

Kings used spices to show off the elaborate meals they could have, making these spices associated with riches and power.

The Arabs' hold as middlemen in the spice trade held out until 1498, when Portuguese explorer Vasco da Gama managed to sail around the southern tip of Africa to reach India for the first time in European history. This started a battle with the Arabs, who were not very happy to relinquish their grip on the spice trade.

Do you know what other famous explorers set sail in an attempt to reach India for spices?

Christopher Columbus was searching for pepper and a route to break into the spice trade when he took a wrong turn.

Without the elusive and luxurious spices from the Far East, global trade and exploration might have never been set in motion, altering history as we know it.

Spices on the Silk Road represented more than just excitement for one's taste buds. The spice trade shaped culinary traditions all along the trade route. Spices also serve as a marker for the transport of knowledge and culture along the Silk Road. Where the spices went, religious and cultural ideas followed, along with massive amounts of wealth.

Today, we can trace spices along the Silk Road based on shared gastronomic heritage. Not only do we find common dishes being made with similar ingredients all up and down the Silk Road, but we can also see common ideas as well. For example, the idea of hot and cold foods from Iran is the same in Chinese culture and is similar to the concept of ayurveda from India. This is a direct result of cultures blending together along the trade route!

Precious Metals and Gems

Speaking of massive amounts of wealth, spices were not the only money-making goods traded along the Silk Road. Accompanying the exotic spices from the Far East were eye-popping gemstones and precious metals that wowed the elite members of society in the West.

Deep in the Hindu Kush Mountains, even still in the present day, lies a mine in such a remote area that it only opens up for a few summer months out of the year. This mine is in Sar-e-Sang, a valley located in present-day Badakhshan, Afghanistan.

The gorgeous gemstone mined in Sar-e-Sang is called lapis lazuli. Greek philosopher Theophrastus, who lived from around 372 to 287

BCE, called lapis lazuli a sapphire spotted with gold.

Removing the deposits of lapis lazuli from deep within the Hindu Kush Mountains was a formidable task for miners. The mine's limestone rocks were so hard that ancient miners had to use fire to crack them in order to remove the gems. Lapis lazuli was mined in large blocks. These blocks were carried out of the mines on the backs of men, then transported by donkey to camps and then to a nearby village. The large blocks were eventually carved for trade.

Today, lapis lazuli is still removed from the mines in the exact same manner, on the backs of men and transported through the rough mountain terrain and high passes on donkeys to the nearest village.

Roman or Greek ring stone made of lapis lazuli.
Metropolitan Museum of Art, CC0, via Wikimedia Commons;
https://commons.wikimedia.org/wiki/File:Lapis_lazuli_ring_stone_MET_DP261442_(cropped).jpg

Lapis lazuli was considered a treasure in the ancient world. It has been found in archaeological sites in many places, including ancient Ur, Neolithic Mesopotamia, Greece, the Roman Empire, Egypt, and China. Lapis lazuli has been found in the tombs of only the wealthiest members of these societies. It was revered for its blue color, and it was used in rituals for many societies, including the Hebrews, Babylonians, and Assyrians.

Perhaps better known to the average person than lapis lazuli is the bright green gemstone called jade. Jade played a major role in diplomatic trade during the Tang dynasty and contributed to the factors that allowed the Silk Road to flourish and grow.

In China, jade was renowned for toolmaking and as a beautiful ritualistic gemstone. For the Chinese, jade represented the five qualities that every man should have: kindness, morality, wisdom, bravery, and purity. Jade was synonymous with the ideals of purity and indestructibility.

The indestructible aspect of jade made it the perfect material for tools in times before smelting and forging were possible. You may have heard of the Bronze Age, which occurred some five thousand years ago. Scholars say there was a lesser-known Jade Age that occurred alongside the Bronze Age in China and as far west as the Mediterranean due to the prevalence of jade toolmaking.

The Chinese exhausted their jade mines; you may be able to guess what happened next.

The route for trade was wide open.

The Chinese located another source of jade in Khotan in the far western part of China, along the Silk Road. Khotan became an important trade hub and a multicultural city. The city was known for being the first area outside of central China to farm mulberry trees, the food for the silkworms used to make silk threads. The people in Khotan also became famous for their carpets, which were as valuable as precious metals.

The trade for jade tools died down when China became a center of advanced bronze technology during the Bronze Age. However, jade remained a nearly sacred gem to Chinese culture throughout its history, and it still continues to play a significant role today.

In the West, we think of gold as the ultimate precious metal. In China and along the Silk Road, gold was valuable, though not as much as jade was, especially in China. Other items held as much, if not more, value than gold, such as silk or gemstones.

Gold and silver were both used as currencies for buying and selling goods on the Silk Road. Because the Silk Road was so long and went between many countries and cultures, it became necessary to exchange currencies between regions. One easy way to do this was by the weight of the gold or silver in a coin.

It did not matter where the coin came from. The value was simply determined by the weight, creating simple currency exchanges that spanned all regions of the Silk Road.

Gold and silver coins are long lasting and do not decay like other items traded along the Silk Road. This has left archaeologists with an amazing trail of evidence when it comes to trade. Gold and silver coins from multiple countries have been found all along the trade route, showing just how far people and their goods (and their coins!) were able to travel.

Coins from the Persian Empire and the Byzantine Empire have been found as far east as China, along with the bodies of foreign traders and foreign officials.

The Chinese were somewhat of an exception to the gold and silver currencies, as they preferred to use jade and silk in trade. Some evidence shows they might have worn gold coins as pendants.

Gold was worn in other Silk Road cultures as well. Gold was woven into silk, embroidered on garments, and, of course, made into jewelry. Gold was used as a symbol of wealth and status, similar to gemstones.

Gold on the Silk Road was mined along the Mediterranean, mainly in North Africa in the Sahara region. From there, the gold was traded for other goods like spices, clothing, silk, and gemstones. The gold then traveled back toward the Far East along the Silk Road, proving just how intricate the web of trade was.

Lapis lazuli was mined in blustery, cold, high-altitude mountains and sent down the Silk Road. In stark contrast, pearls were gathered from the warm Persian Gulf and joined the precious lapis lazuli on the trade route as a luxury item for the rich. Exceptionally high-quality pearls have been mentioned as far back as ancient Mesopotamia. They have also been found as far as India, central Asia, China, and Europe.

Overall, the cultural significance of both gemstones and precious metals that were mined and traded along the Silk Road was immeasurable. Alongside silk, gemstones and precious metals powered the diplomatic advances in regions of the Silk Road, paving the way for further trade and expansion.

Other Valuable Goods

Thus far, we have mentioned quite a few important trade goods on the Silk Road, such as silk, spices, gems, and precious metals. The Silk Road was like a one-stop shop, a large trade hub for everything you could possibly imagine (at least everything that could travel in a caravan or on a boat between remote regions).

Today, when we say the word porcelain, what comes to mind? For some of us, it will be the porcelain throne or the toilet. For others, we will think of fine china on a fancy table. During the time of the Silk Road, people associated porcelain with the country of China because the Chinese were prolific producers of these hard, translucent ceramics.

The porcelain trade began during the Tang dynasty during the initial expansion of the Silk Road. It started out as fine tableware and decorative items but soon expanded to gorgeous decorations and unique artwork produced by massive kilns during the Ming dynasty.

The love for porcelain spread along the Silk Road, and Chinese culture and artwork spread along with it. Chinese porcelain pottery had intricate designs that blended with the artwork of other cultures since the pottery was traded and shared from region to region.

For a number of years, the Chinese closely guarded their porcelain-making methods, similar to the way they kept the secret about silk's true origins. Eventually, other cultures learned how to make their own porcelain. The Persians had their own style of ceramics that was heavily influenced by Chinese porcelain.

What do you think people were drinking out of their fine porcelain cups? If you immediately thought of tea, you would be correct! Tea leaves were yet another famous good traded along the Silk Road.

Once again, our journey begins deep within China, this time around 2737 BCE. At some point during this legendary year, Emperor Shennong was minding his own business while boiling some water underneath a tree.

As fate would have it, a few leaves from a *Camellia sinensis* plant nearby were knocked off by a gust of wind and landed right into his pot of boiling water.

The result was quite a surprise. It had a pleasant taste, and as legend goes, it also had medicinal properties. This was the first pot of tea ever made.

From this point on, tea was cultivated from the leaves of the *Camellia sinensis* plant. From the 16th to the 3rd century BCE, the Chinese perfected the cultivation of tea leaves, and they began transporting dried leaves around the region. During the Tang dynasty, tea exploded in popularity, and tea houses opened for business.

At this point, tea leaves began to travel down the Silk Road, spreading into other nearby cultures. Eventually, tea became an internationally known beverage. The sweet tea people drink today in the southern United States would never have been possible if tea had not taken a journey down the Silk Road!

There was one more very important item that traveled down the Silk Road that completely changed history as we know it. Yes, furs, livestock, textiles, foods, and even slaves were traded on the Silk Road, but what about paper?

The Chinese yet again burst onto the scene with a world-shattering discovery: papermaking.

The earliest Chinese paper was made with materials like mulberry bark, bamboo, and hemp, which were pounded into a pulp, moistened with water, and spread thin to dry.

At first, paper was a luxury reserved only for important official documents, writings, and special artwork. Over time, paper mills were established across China, making paper more common and accessible.

Initially, paper on the Silk Road was a novel concept. It soon caught on, as scholars began writing down their knowledge and sharing it from city to city along the Silk Road.

Religious texts were also shared through paper. In 751 CE, Arabs captured Chinese prisoners of war during the Battle of Talas. It is believed this was the first time papermaking knowledge reached the Muslims. The Islamic world was particularly fond of paper, taking the Chinese method and adding cotton and linen fibers to create something softer and more pliable.

Paper changed the world in obvious ways. Knowledge could now be written down in books and shared across wide distances. Paper was perfectly suited for travel on a trade route. It was not until the 12th century that the Muslims in Spain created their own paper mills, allowing the knowledge of papermaking to spread across Europe.

Paper, porcelain, and tea leaves traveled from Asia along the Silk Road to Europe, but what was coming back to Asia in return? The Chinese valued wool and woven textiles from Europe for their good quality. Horses were traded between the two regions as well. Herbs, which were used for their medicinal properties, were also imported to China from Europe along the Silk Road. Wine from Rome was sent to the East. Precious metals like gold and silver were also traded, along with amber that was sourced from Europe.

Chapter 5: The Travelers of the Silk Road

Perhaps the most famous European traveler along the Silk Road is Marco Polo. His fame lay in doing exactly what most travelers on the Silk Road did not do. That is, he allegedly traveled the entire route from start to finish.

Instead, the average traveler would only go a short distance from place to place, from city to city, or from trading point to trading point. Many of these people were just traders who moved goods from one place to the next and took their cut out of the price.

In some situations, people created entire caravans to travel as a group. This was often for protection against attack and theft. Caravans were most commonly used to cross the desert regions of the Silk Road for strength in numbers.

Let us take a look at what might have gone into creating an ancient Silk Road caravan.

First, we have to consider that not all caravans were exactly the same. The contents of the caravan varied widely depending on the destination, the goods they were carrying, and a number of other factors.

Let us say we were organizing a caravan through the desert. We would take Bactrian camels as our main source of transportation.

Bactrian camels have two humps and two coats of hair. The first coat of hair is the outer layer that faces the elements. The second coat of hair is the inner layer that protects the skin. This layer of hair should never get wet. The space between the two layers creates a pocket of air that holds warmth or protects the body from heat, making these camels ideal for travel in extreme climates like the desert, where it could be hot during the day and very cold at night.

These impressive beasts also have two sets of eyelids and eyelashes to protect them against sandstorms and desert dust. The second set of eyelids functions as a sort of windshield wiper, smoothing away debris during a sandstorm. The camel's nostrils can shrink down to narrow slits during sandstorms to protect the lungs from choking on sand.

The Bactrian camel has other special features that allow it to travel long distances across inhospitable deserts. These hardy camels can go up to one week without any water and up to a month without food!

The secret lies within their two humps. The humps store up to one hundred pounds of fat each! When the humps are full to the brim with fat, they can rise eighteen inches off of the camel's body. As the fat stores are used up, the humps shrink down lower and lower.

In our caravan through the desert, we would tie at least two camels or maybe more, possibly up to six of them, together, nose to tail.

The camels will be carefully loaded with the goods we want to trade or sell. Camels are grumpy creatures and will complain if they are uncomfortable, so we would need to load them just right. To load the goods, we would use some cargo racks or baskets that we tie on with blankets to the camel's backs.

Riding on the first camel is our caravan leader. This person is a man who has several important qualities. First, he is a skilled guide who knows his way through the sand dunes. He knows the location of hidden wells and outposts along the way. He does not use a map or a compass. Instead, he travels by following familiar routes and landmarks and using the North Star as a guide. He knows our camels prefer to go across the tops of the dunes rather than waste energy going up and down them.

Second, he is a skilled talker. He is great at negotiating and trading.

As for those of us in the caravan, we might walk sometimes. Later, we will climb on the camels' shoulders to ride. Some of us will bring horses. The wind is so strong in the desert that we will not talk much. We will have a cloth over our noses and mouths to keep blowing sand out.

We will travel through the hot day until after dark when it begins to get cold. Then, we will stop to unload the camels so they can rest. To keep the camels from wandering off, we will hobble their feet with rope. Once the camels are unloaded, someone will build a fire, and we will cook whatever we have brought along on the journey to eat—probably some stew or grains boiled over the flames or maybe some onions, peppers, or goat meat we got at the last oasis stop.

In the morning, we will eat the leftovers for breakfast before loading up the camels again and continuing on our journey. We brought some dates to eat for lunch while riding.

Riding in a caravan was not as easy as it sounds here. We have to keep the camels moving at the exact same pace, or they will tangle their ropes and break them, creating a disaster. The last thing we would want is a runaway camel carrying precious cargo in the middle of the sand dunes.

We also have to constantly be on the lookout for bandits who are looking to steal our goods, our coins, or even our camels.

We brought grass with us, which we use to sleep on at night and feed to the camels. We find camel ticks crawling on us and biting us, which is very unpleasant.

When we reach an oasis in the desert, the camels find palm fronds or scrubby trees to munch on. They can drink twenty-five to thirty gallons of water in one sitting!

When we reach a caravanserai, we feel excitement and relief. We see a set of buildings with a courtyard full of animals tied out on wooden stakes and a covered market area.

This is a stopping place on the Silk Road. There is an inn to sleep in, a stable for our animals, and plenty of food and water. We are going to spend about a week resting here before tackling the rest of our long journey. We need the camels and horses to fatten up a little bit.

This place also has a lot of people to trade with. There are brothels here, people from multiple different cultures, and impressive market stalls to shop in. We can sleep at the inn, and we have to pay a fee for our animals to stay in the stable and eat. The owners collect the manure from our animals to sell as fuel or compost, which allows the courtyard to stay clean.

Eventually, we will move on and travel through the desert again for a few days until we reach the next stop along our route.

Who Traveled the Silk Road?

A camel caravan.
https://commons.wikimedia.org/wiki/File:Richard_Zommer_-
Camel_Caravan_with_Travelling_Family.jpg

Those who made the perilous journeys along the Silk Road came from a wide variety of backgrounds. Some were simply tradesmen who lived in the area and regularly traveled from one trade point to the next. These were the middlemen who were responsible for changing goods from hand to hand along the route.

Scholars traveled along the trade routes for a variety of reasons. If a scholar was in search of a certain religious text, he would have to journey along the Silk Road in order to find it.

Some people took pilgrimages to sacred religious sites. This included Hindus, Buddhists, Christians, and Muslims, among others.

Scholars who studied different cultures and religions would travel the Silk Road in search of new people and places to observe and document. These scholars contributed mightily to the exchange of cross-cultural ideas.

Many caravanserais were meeting places for scholars to spend time sharing their ideas in person so they could learn from each other. They wrote together, shared poetry and stories, held debates, and pooled together results from studies they had conducted. Scholars also traveled the Silk Road to study botany, astronomy, and geographical features, which they also shared with each other at meeting points along the route.

Artists would draw what they saw along the route and observe the different cultures they came into contact with along the way. Philosophers gained new insights and shared them with others. Translators were able to get their hands on different manuscripts and rewrite them in other languages so that ideas could be shared with even more cultures.

The Silk Road played a vital role in the spread of knowledge and ideas, creating a melting pot of knowledge and culture for people to partake in.

While most people know of Marco Polo, few have heard about Abu Abdullah Muhammad Ibn Battuta. Commonly known as Ibn Battuta, he was a young man born in Tangier, Morocco, on February 24th, 1304 CE.

A sketch of what Ibn Battuta might have looked like.
https://commons.wikimedia.org/wiki/File:Ibn_Battuta,_Sayr_mulhimah_min_al-Sharq_wa-al-Gharb.png

Ibn Battuta was a scholar who set out to travel the Silk Road in search of knowledge. He was gone on his journey for more than thirty years. During his travels, which took place from 1325 to 1354, Islam was expanding rapidly outside of modern-day Saudia Arabia, with religious ideas traveling along the Silk Road and into outlying territories.

Ibn Battuta first traveled to Mecca as a religious pilgrimage for his Muslim faith. He journeyed to Algiers and Tunis in North Africa. He also went to Egypt, where he visited twenty-two different cities, including Cairo and Alexandria. He then traveled through Palestine and Syria in the Middle East before eventually reaching Mecca in the Arabian Peninsula.

During his trip, he documented everything and made observations about his experiences. He was known as the Muslim traveling judge and a legal scholar.

His travels were not purely religious. Ibn Battuta wanted to find knowledge and visit libraries. He dreamed of going to the libraries of Cairo, Alexandria, and Damascus.

In Tunis (or possibly Mecca), he became a paid judge called a qadi, who traveled with caravans to settle their disputes. Ibn Battuta traveled to many different regions, living his life to the fullest. He married at least ten times during his travels and fathered multiple children while traveling along the Silk Road.

He journeyed through the Hindu Kush Mountains to reach India, where he asked the king of India for an official career. He became a judge of Delhi, but he grew bored after eight years. Ibn Battuta got the king of India to make him an ambassador to China, allowing him to continue his travels along the Silk Road.

Once Ibn Battuta returned home some thirty years later, he wrote a book detailing his adventures. It was titled *The Travels of Ibn Battuta: In the Near East, Asia and Africa.*

Who else traveled along the Silk Road?

Well, soldiers frequented the Silk Road for a number of reasons. First and foremost, soldiers would be sent to guard important caravans against bandits or rival tribes.

Soldiers were used as police of sorts to guard the caravanserais or settlements against chaos since tired and hungry people from a wide range of backgrounds all came together in one place.

The soldiers were also given the task of collecting taxes and checking for smugglers in some regions. Of course, one might also find soldiers traveling the Silk Road for average military purposes. They went between regions during battles and to prepare for incoming threats. Military outposts were established at various points along the Silk Road by local governments so they could have prepared military bases when they were needed.

There was another group of people that often traveled the Silk Road: slaves.

Arguably, slaves could be called one of the world's oldest currencies. The Silk Road was also referred to as the Slave Road for good reason.

Slaves during the time of the Silk Road were used for many purposes. They were often used as laborers for agriculture and farming or for domestic labor in rich households. When big projects were under way, like the construction of a new canal or bridge, slaves were brought in to help complete the project. Slaves were sometimes prisoners of war. Women and children could be slaves; they were often captured when a settlement was seized. Slaves also filled the brothels in caravanserais and city settlements.

From the 7th to the 9th century CE, it is estimated that 80 percent of caravans had slaves. It has also been recently estimated that 39 percent of travelers on the Silk Road in central Asia were traveling as slaves.[14] Most of these slaves were children from impoverished families.

Historians and archaeologists are still learning more about human trafficking on the Silk Road in ancient times. Recently, slaveholder contracts have been found in tombs in the Turfan region. The Turfan region was an ancient oasis city on the Silk Road in the present-day Xinjiang region of China. These contracts give historians clues about the ages of slaves on the Silk Road, as well as whether they were male or female.

The greatest slave trade in history occurred on the Silk Road when the Mongols transported Caucasians, Tartars, and Slavs to Crimea on the Black Sea to be sold as slaves.

Human trafficking is a lesser talked about but very important "good" traded on the Silk Road. Enslaved people were just as valued as silk, paper, and gemstones. In fact, regional governments that profited from import taxes on basic goods like silk and spices also taxed slaves in the same manner.

Human trafficking was present on the Silk Road for the entirety of its history. Even in the Middle Ages, a significant number of Europeans were trafficked along the Silk Road in exchange for silver. The slave trade was a booming business all across the spine of Asia and into Africa and Europe for thousands of years, operating as a hidden thread that boosted the wealth of empires on the Silk Road.

---

[14] "Slave Trade on the Silk Road." https://shanghai.nyu.edu/news/exploring-silk-road-slave-trade-turfan.

In the end, when we look back at our timeline of history and view the bigger picture, the travelers of the Silk Road were more than just random people who participated in trade. They were important to the culture and history of many regions, some traveling willingly and others traveling by force. However, each person participated in shaping the religions and cultures of many places in central Asia for centuries.

Chapter 6: The Silk Road: Art and Architecture

The Silk Road is home to thousands of years of human history. Some of the many clues left behind for historians and archaeologists are sealed in tombs or written down in surviving manuscripts. Other valuable insights have been left behind for us to explore in the form of buildings and artwork.

The architecture left along the Silk Road gives us information about the values of the people who lived in the area and tells the story of how they lived their daily lives.

Some aspects of architecture on the Silk Road are the same in every place, regardless of the culture and the location. This is because the architecture was designed to meet a specific need of the travelers. The finer details of aesthetics, such as the materials used and the style, were left up to the local culture.

Caravanserais

Caravanserais, the places created along the Silk Road for travelers to rest their animals and sleep, are all arranged in the exact same manner no matter where they are located on the trade route. Each location consisted of a circle of buildings with a courtyard in the center for animals.

A caravanserai in Iran.

We know that many of the cities that developed along the Silk Road were originally oases and trade hubs. They grew over time into large, prosperous cities due to the economic benefits of trade.

Palmyra, a city that blossomed in the middle of the desolate Tadmorean Desert, is one such city. In the present day, the ruins of Palmyra's Silk Road architecture can be found in Syria. Unfortunately, recent wars have brought unknown amounts of destruction to many of these historic ruins.

Palmyra is a true caravan city, growing out of a crisscross of caravan trails in no-man's land. The initial infrastructure of this desert oasis was developed to meet the needs of people who were passing through the area on the Silk Road. Palmyra had a public meeting place in the city center known as the agora, which was probably built during the 1st century. The style of the agora matches the architecture of other Greco-Roman cities.[15]

The buildings of Palmyra were constructed from beautiful pale gold limestone gathered from the local landscape. The market, built for trade as travelers passed through, had a magnificent colonnade. The colonnade

---

[15] https://en.unesco.org/silkroad/content/palmyra

had around 375 columns that were 31 feet (9.5 meters) in height.

The artwork found in Palmyra gives further evidence of Greek and Roman influence over this Middle Eastern city. Sculptures match the Greek style of the time period. Greek and Parthian clothing styles have been found in the ruins of Palmyra.

The Greek clothing for men included a long linen tunic with a cloth that went down to the elbows and a large cloak made of linen or wool. Archaeologists also discovered remnants of Chinese silk.

The Parthian clothing was different. It included a long-sleeved tunic worn with pants that were tight around the ankles. Parthian clothing was also worn with a cloak over the top and included a belt and boots. The cloth had ornate patterns, setting it apart from the Greek style.

Palmyra was most certainly a multicultural city with its gorgeous architecture and various clothing styles. The Greek influence was heavy, as caravans often filtered into Palmyra from the west. Inscriptions inside the architecture and in the graveyard were in several languages, such as Greek and Aramaic. In later years, they were also in Latin.

Mosques

Another fabulous example of architecture and art spreading from region to region via the Silk Road is the Hagia Sophia in Istanbul, Turkey, with its massive 180-foot dome. First built in 532 by Emperor Justinian, it was the largest Christian church in the world for quite some time.

A photo of Hagia Sophia from 2013.
Arild Vågen, CC BY-SA 3.0 <https://creativecommons.org/licenses/by-sa/3.0>, via Wikimedia Commons; https://commons.wikimedia.org/wiki/File:Hagia_Sophia_Mars_2013.jpg

After the Ottomans conquered the area and converted the Hagia Sophia into a mosque in 1453, they added four minarets to the mosque. Visitors from all over came to visit the Hagia Sophia and saw its splendor before traveling to other regions.[16]

The Sultanahmet Mosque was built nearby in the same style, with a dome and four minarets. Silk Road trade is evident in this mosque as well because of the twenty thousand blue-painted İznik tiles in the interior, which first gained popularity when people traveled the Silk Road years before.

What is unique about these handmade blue tiles?

The Mongols, led by one Genghis Khan, reached neighboring Iran in 1220. With them came Chinese art and architecture, including knowledge of ceramic making.

The people of Constantinople had gained a taste for fine Chinese ceramics. Soon, they began trading ceramics with China. During the Ming dynasty, the famous blue and white Ming porcelains heavily influenced the design of the blue İznik tiles inside the Sultanahmet Mosque.

This mosque was built in the same style as the previous mosques, with a dome and minarets. It even included the color blue, which represented water. The blue exterior became a key feature of Persian domes.

Persian Islamic design influenced mosques all along the Silk Road, but the architecture of the mosques was not the only feature that spread from city to city. Impressive gardens were also popular and could be found accompanying beautiful architecture up and down the Silk Road.

In present-day southeast Uzbekistan, weary Silk Road travelers found the city of Samarkand. The Bibi-Khanym Mosque in Samarkand has a massive dome that was built using ninety-five elephants from India. It was finished in 1404. This mosque had eight minarets and a three-walled turquoise blue dome with a tiled interior.

We can follow the unbroken link of the Silk Road by looking at the architecture from place to place. For instance, the Bibi-Khanym Mosque was a direct influence on the design of perhaps the most famous building in India: the Taj Mahal in Agra.

---

[16] https://www.saga.co.uk/magazine/travel/destinations/asia/central-asia/silk-road-islamic-architecture

Hints of Istanbul and Samarkand can be clearly seen in India when viewing the Taj Mahal, but let us not forget about the gardens! The Taj Mahal also has a large garden divided into four segments, just like the gardens of Persia. Each garden features shade and running water. These gardens were supposed to remind people of paradise.

The Taj Mahal has a large water feature with a carefully designed reflection that creates symmetry. The gardens of the Taj Mahal resemble the gardens of Samarkand, with their division into quarters and a pavilion in the center.

The Silk Road's influence spanned thousands of miles, even reaching into far eastern China, where mosques began to appear. However, the Chinese mosques were not domed. They had more of a Buddhist style of architecture.

The Great Mosque of Xi'an was built using local wood and has a single three-story minaret in an octagonal shape. At first glance, a traveler may not see the link to the domed mosques of the Middle East. But take a closer look, and you will find that the unbroken chain of influence along the Silk Road still stands strong. The prayer hall has a roof made with glazed turquoise tile, giving a nod to the blue tiles of the domed mosques in Samarkand and beyond.

Stupas

Take a leap backward on our timeline of history, a time before Islam and mosques came through the Silk Road. Buddhist stupas were prevalent on the trade route, first emerging from India and spreading east into China. Each stupa and its artwork left behind clues to the places people traveled based on its architectural influence and inscriptions.

You may be wondering what a stupa is, especially if you live in the Western Hemisphere. Stupa is the Sanskrit word for *heap*. The first stupas were simply burial mounds containing a bit of the Buddha's ashes.

Over time, stupa architecture expanded to be burial mounds with rocks. India's King Ashoka (r. 269–232 BCE) built more than eighty-four thousand stupas all over India, Nepal, Pakistan, Bangladesh, and Afghanistan.

The Great Stupa (Mahastupa) was built at the birthplace of King Ashoka's wife, Devi. It was located along a major Silk Road trade route in Madya Pradesh, India.

The Great Stupa at Sanchi.

The stupa has a domed roof, which predates the spread of Islam and the domed mosques. Unlike the mosques, the stupa is not meant to be entered. It is a solid mound that a person walks around.

The southern route of the Silk Road along the Tarim Basin in northwestern China had stupas with northwestern Indian architectural features. That is quite a long distance for knowledge and ideas to travel!

Buddhist statues give us more clues as to the influence of art on the Silk Road. The Bamiyan Valley is an isolated region high in the Hindu Kush Mountains of Afghanistan. This area became a major link along the Silk Road between India and China.

There, archaeologists discovered ancient Buddhist statues with blatant evidence of influence from the trade route. The Kushans who lived in this area became middlemen in the trade between China, India, and Rome. They seamlessly blended their tribal culture with their trade partners, leaving behind an unforgettable cultural legacy.

The central Asian traditions fused with Hellenistic art from the Greek Mediterranean region, and this blended into Buddhist religious practices coming out of India.

Evidence of this is clearly shown in the art and statues left behind. The Buddha statues of Bamiyan display Roman clothing. A stupa called Tope Darra (or Topdara), located in the mountains north of Kabul, contains statues with Hellenistic features.

In 2001, the Taliban destroyed two large Buddha figures from the 5th century outside of Bamiyan. These two statues stood together in cliffside niches, with artificially created caves surrounding them in the cliffs. Inside the caves were artistic influences from India and Iran, along with Hellenistic art and Greek influences.

The chain of influence from the Silk Road spread smoothly from tribe to tribe and from region to region as items were traded between people groups over the trade route, leaving behind artwork displaying a fascinating fusion of cultures.

In 970 CE, Bamiyan was conquered by the Muslims, and Islam arrived in the region. The blend of religious and cultural influences continued for hundreds of years as domed stupas gave way to domed mosques.

Ancient pagoda in Sidoktaya.

In addition to stupas, the Buddhists also created Chinese pagodas. These evolved out of stupas. Pagodas were larger buildings that could be entered, unlike the stupas, which were mounds containing relics that could only be circled by visitors. Both pagodas and stupas were memorials to pay respect to the famous and important Buddhists who had died, including the Buddha himself.

In Xi'an, China, the famous Big Wild Goose Pagoda still stands. It was first built in 652 CE during the Tang dynasty and then rebuilt in 704. It climbs seven stories high.

Do you know what the main function of this pagoda was and still is today? The pagoda holds statues of Gautama Buddha, which were brought back to China by a man named Xuanzang in the 7th century. He was a scholar, traveler, and translator. These statues of Buddha are renowned in China, and they traveled along the Silk Road from India.

Statue of Xuanzang in front of Big Wild Goose Pagoda.
John Hill, CC BY-SA 4.0 <https://creativecommons.org/licenses/by-sa/4.0>, via Wikimedia Commons; https://commons.wikimedia.org/wiki/File:Statue_of_Xuanzang_in_front_of_Giant_Wild_Goose_P agoda._Xi%27an._2011.jpg

Today, Big Wild Goose Pagoda is a World Heritage Site. It was added in 2014 as part of the "Silk Roads: The Routes Network of Chang'an-Tianshan Corridor," which aims to preserve the heritage of the Silk Road in the Chang'an-Tianshan region of the route. There are thirty-three sites along the route, which spans more than 3,106 miles (5,000 kilometers) through China, Kazakhstan, and Kyrgyzstan.

Other regions along the Silk Road are also identified as World Heritage Sites, with each region made up of countries that submit applications for sites to UNESCO for approval.

Mogao Caves

The Mogao Caves.

Even Buddhist cave art has elements of other regions incorporated into it. The Mogao Caves, also known as the Thousand Buddha Grottoes or Caves of the Thousand Buddhas, are located in what was an oasis of the Silk Road in present-day Gansu Province, China, outside of the city of Dunhuang. This crossroads was a place where many cultures mixed together, as evidenced by the artwork inside of the caves.

It is estimated that the artwork inside of the caves spans more than one thousand years of history. These caves were dug out, so they are fully manmade, not natural caves. The first cave was dug out in 366 CE, with construction of the caves continuing all the way until the 14th century! Today, there remain more than five hundred connected temples inside of the cave system.

These caves were used for worship and meditation by Buddhists who lived and traveled in the region. The most amazing aspect of the Mogao

Caves is the artwork contained within them. These caves have more than 400,000 square feet of frescos and sculptures. In fact, there is so much art in the caves that it covers ten major genres, including architecture, stucco sculpture, wall paintings, silk paintings, calligraphy, woodblock printing, embroidery, literature, music, and dance.

A cave mural of Zhang Qian traveling along the Silk Road.
https://commons.wikimedia.org/wiki/File:Zhang_Qian.jpg

The cave murals display rich, intricate artwork and fill cave chambers from floor to ceiling. The influence of Buddhist artwork can be clearly seen in the cave paintings. The earliest paintings display characteristics from India and central Asia in the painting style and clothing worn in the portraits. However, a distinct local painting style began to emerge, blending together cultures.

The Mogao Caves also contain unique architecture. You may not think of a cave system as having architectural features, but these caves certainly do. The earliest caves are similar to rock-cut caves found in India, like the Ajanta Caves. This style features a square central column with cut-outs meant to hold sculptures. This style represents the stupa architecture since visitors were supposed to walk in a circle around the memorial statues.

Another type of architectural design found in the cave system is hall caves. These caves had pyramid-shaped ceilings meant to resemble a tent. Some of them had flat carved ceilings resembling that of a building.

The third architectural type represented in the caves is the vihara cave plan, which was the monastery style from India. These caves were used for meditation. Each one contains side chambers that are only large enough for one person to sit inside to meditate.

The city of Dunhuang itself is a strategic point on the intricate web of trade routes. It lay at a crossroads between two major trade routes of the Silk Road. It sits on an oasis in the Taklamakan Desert, poised against Crescent Lake and Mingsha Shan on the western edge of the Gobi Desert. In Chinese, Mingsha Shan means "Singing Sand Mountain." This site was named after the singing noise made by the wind hitting the sand dunes in the desert.

Imagine traveling through the desert and arriving at this oasis city. As your exhausted caravan pulls closer to the town, you are anxious to see China for the first time (Dunhuang was the first Chinese city travelers encountered on the Silk Road when coming from India in the west). All you can hear is the sound of the dunes singing in the whipping desert wind.

The first part of the city you would reach is the Jade Gate, a garrison erected to protect this important trade city from invaders. Inside the gates, you find a melting pot of humanity. Tradesmen, Buddhist scholars, and craftsmen all meet here.

Dunhuang produced a number of goods to sell or trade on the Silk Road. It was a big producer of silk and not just one type of silk either. The people there produced several different varieties. The city also had cotton and wool from the surrounding regions. The people used these textiles and created beautiful embroidery. They also produced and sold furs, tea leaves, various medicines, jade objects, camels, sheep, dried fruits, dyes, and tools.

The city was full of different languages, thanks to the tradesmen coming in from the Silk Road. Scrolls found in the library cave of the Mogao Caves give us clues about the people who passed through the city. Chinese and Tibetan were regularly spoken in the city. Sanskrit, Khotanese, Uighur, and Sogdian were also used.

The scrolls also hint that Dunhuang was a city where multiple religions lived side by side. The main religion was Buddhism, but Judaism, Zoroastrianism, Manichaeism, Christianity, and Daoism were also part of the city's vibrant culture.

Outside of China, there are quite a few other UNESCO World Heritage Sites on the Silk Road that people can visit today. Many of these sites have been damaged or destroyed due to weather, earthquakes, and wars. Work is being done by many countries around the world to preserve what is left of the unique cultural heritage left behind by the Silk Road.

Chapter 7: Religion and the Silk Road

Religion along the Silk Road was continually fluid, spreading in ripples and waves and blending with local tribal traditions. Different faiths often coexisted side by side in multicultural oasis cities, but more often than not, religions competed with each other until a winner took over and swept along the Silk Road, bringing with it the artistic and architectural influences we discussed in the previous chapter.

Zoroastrianism

This ancient religion was said to be the precursor to the three major Abrahamic religions: Judaism, Christianity, and Islam. Many consider it the father of monotheistic religion.

Zoroaster was one of the first documented people to reject the idea of multiple gods and instead placed faith in one singular god. His god was known as Ahura Mazda, or the Lord of Wisdom. He believed there was an evil force at work in the universe called Ahriman.

Zoroaster was born sometime between the 11th and 6th century BCE in the region of Mongolia and Azerbaijan, but it was not until well after his death in the 3rd century that Zoroastrianism became the official religion of the region when Iran was ruled by the Sasanian dynasty in the Persian Empire.

Zoroastrianism spread down the Silk Road. The religion also made it into the philosophies and teachings of Hellenistic Greece. Though the Greeks had secondhand information that was sometimes incorrect, it is remarkable that Zoroaster's influence was strong enough to appear in writings from classical Greek philosophers several centuries later.

Herodotus, who lived from 484 to 425 BCE, was known as the "Father of History." He wrote about Zoroaster in his book titled *Histories.* Herodotus noted that Zoroaster was a teacher of wisdom and wrote about him as a historical figure who impacted Persian religions.

The Hellenistic Greek geographer Strabo (64-24 CE) wrote about Zoroaster in his work *Geographica* (*Geography*), saying he was a religious leader and philosopher.

At one point in time, a fellow scholar accused Plato of plagiarizing the work of Zoroaster, though no proof has ever been found.

Pliny the Elder was a Roman author and naturalist who lived from 23 to 79 CE. He also wrote about Zoroaster in a similar context to Herodotus, noting that Zoroaster was influential in Persian religions and was a wise teacher. He also goes as far as to name Zoroaster as the inventor of magic, a wild claim that took hold and spread along the Silk Road. It is believed that Zoroaster inspired the Chaldean doctrines of astrology and magic.

A work attributed to Zoroaster about astronomy and predictions that contained five papyrus rolls was also in circulation at some point during the classical Greek and Roman periods.

Despite these claims and what amounts to ancient rumors that have lasted through the ages, all of the talk of magic and astronomy has very little to do with actual Zoroastrianism.

During the time of influential Zoroastrianism, there were many overlaps with other religions found in cultures along the Silk Road. For example, both Zoroastrianism and Hinduism use fire for their rituals.

Many other religions that evolved during the same time period overlapped with Zoroastrianism. The theory of duality—that is, a world with both good and evil—was a major feature of Zoroastrianism and the Abrahamic religions.

Zoroastrianism has persisted to the present day despite being marginalized by the spread of Judaism, Christianity, and Islam on the Silk Road. Today, there are isolated pockets of Zoroastrians in Iran, as well as descendants of Persian immigrants in India, where they are known as Parsis or Parsees. The number of adherents to Zoroastrianism totals around 100,000 to 200,000 people worldwide.

Christianity

During the 1ˢᵗ and 2ⁿᵈ centuries CE, small pockets of Christianity began to appear on the Silk Road. The religion did not travel in a steady wave; rather, it ebbed and flowed, working its way into local religions and slowly pushing out other beliefs.

The Apostle Thomas wrote about his travels to India. He might have also reached other parts of Asia. It is very likely Thomas was one of the Silk Road travelers. Christianity was spread by missionaries who purposefully traveled to spread the gospel far and wide.

Nestorian Christians were some of the first Christians to establish themselves along the Silk Road.[17] This branch of Christianity was slightly different from the mainstream Christianity most of us know today. They had several major theological differences, including the belief that Jesus had a divine nature and a human nature. Known as the Church of the East, they had their own hierarchy separate from the Byzantine and Roman Christian churches.

Archaeologists discovered significant proof that early Christianity was present in China during the Tang dynasty. The Nestorian Stele in Xi'an, China, is a stone monument standing thirty feet (nine meters) tall with an inscription describing the arrival of early Christianity in China. The inscription is written in two languages: Chinese and Syriac. Syriac was a form of Aramaic used in ancient China.

The stele also depicts crosses in intricately carved stone. It tells the story of how Christianity arrived in China. Surprisingly, it was not brought along the Silk Road. Christianity was brought to China by a Persian missionary named Alopen.

Are you surprised that Christianity arrived in China all the way from Persia?

Another surprising factoid is that the emperor of the Tang dynasty, Taizong, is thanked in the inscription for the support and patronage he pledged when the Christian community was established in China. The stele can still be viewed today in Xi'an, China; it is housed in the Xi'an Stele Forest Museum.

---

[17] https://factsanddetails.com/china/cat2/sub90/entry-8324.html

Perhaps one of the most pivotal roles in the spread of Christianity was played by Roman Emperor Constantine the Great. Under previous Roman emperors, Christians had been persecuted. Constantine enacted the Edict of Milan in 313 CE, along with his co-ruler, Licinius. Constantine ruled the eastern half of Rome, and Licinius ruled the western half. Together, they agreed on religious tolerance for the empire as a whole.

This edict ended all persecution of Christians and granted religious tolerance to Christianity in the Roman Empire. Thus, the previously unwelcomed religion of Christianity pivoted from a persecuted sect of people to an acceptable religion within the Roman Empire, paving the way for Christianity to explode from west to east along the Silk Road.

Islam

Christianity was present in multiple communities along the Silk Road by the 1st century CE, although it would take a few hundred years for the religion to truly become popular with people. Several centuries later, Islam stormed the scene. The Prophet Muhammad began sharing his teachings in the Arabian Peninsula in the 7th century CE.

The Silk Road is almost entirely responsible for the spread of Islam throughout the world. Arabs were known for their sailing skills. If you remember when we discussed the spice trade in a previous chapter, you will know that the Arabs had a corner on that market. They came up with fantastical stories to trick their customers, hiding the true origin of the spices they sold.

When Islam took hold of the Arabian Peninsula in the 7th century CE, those Arab sailors were also affected. As they followed the maritime Silk Road trade routes into the Far East to buy spices, they stopped at ports along the way, where they shared information about the Prophet Muhammad.

The traders also brought their new religion to the Spice Islands along the coast of India, where they bought and traded rare spices to bring to the West. Inevitably, some of the merchants stayed in Indonesia to live with the local people, establishing Islam as a religion on the island.

Nearby Sumatra and the Philippines were influenced in the same manner. The king of Sumatra converted to Islam in the 12th century CE, and tombstones have been found with Islamic inscriptions by the 13th century.[18] Islam was the first monotheistic religion to take hold in the Philippines.[19]

Today, Islam is the second most widely practiced religion in the Philippines; Christianity is the most popular religion. Islam is mainly concentrated in the Bangsamoro region of the islands, where around 91 percent of the people are Sunni Muslims, though Muslims only make up around 6 percent of the total population of the Philippines.

Further commerce along the Silk Road also brought Brunei and Malaysia into the Islamic fold. Islam began to spread quickly through these eastern islands.

However, not every interaction with Islam on the Silk Road was peaceful. Over a few hundred years, Islam spread like wildfire from the Arabian Peninsula, north to India, and as far west as Spain.

During the 7th century CE, Arab Muslim armies began conquering vast amounts of territory. They managed to take over the Byzantines. It only took twenty years for the Arabs to take over three continents, bringing Muslim rule to a large portion of the Silk Road.

During the Umayyad dynasty, which lasted from 661 to 750 CE, and the Abbasid dynasty, which lasted from 750 to 1250 CE, Islamic and Arabic culture really began to take hold and grow in the newly conquered territories. This was partially because a centralized political state developed. Tribal leaders were replaced by one main monarch, who fully united the territory both politically and religiously. Arabic became the main language, which helped to establish a national identity.

Under the rule of the Abbasid dynasty, the Islamic Golden Age began, which carried on through the 13th century. Religious scholars taught in prestigious institutions, arts flourished, and knowledge spread. There were also many conversions to Islam.

Islamic architecture left a long-lasting impact on the Silk Road that still continues to this day. Remember the domed mosques and minarets we spoke about in the previous chapter? And do not forget about the blue tiles that were influenced by the blue and white porcelain from the Ming dynasty, which led to a legacy of blue-domed mosques all across the

---

[18] https://slate.com/news-and-politics/2005/01/how-islam-got-to-the-philippines.html

[19] https://en.wikipedia.org/wiki/Islam_in_the_Philippines

world.

Scholars from the Islamic Golden Age also left a lasting impression on the West. For example, we do not typically use Roman numerals to write our numbers. We use the Arabic style of writing, which was developed by Islamic scholars and spread westward with trade and cultural exchange.

Many popular works of poetry and literature emerged during this time period. The famous *One Thousand and One Nights*, also often known as *Arabian Nights*, is just one example. This set of stories includes "Aladdin's Wonderful Lamp," "Ali Baba and the Forty Thieves," and "Sinbad the Sailor." These stories have been retold and remastered time and time again throughout history.

Hinduism and Buddhism

Both Hinduism and Buddhism originated in the country of India. They spread in pockets along the Silk Road over hundreds of years and left a legacy of architectural and artistic history.

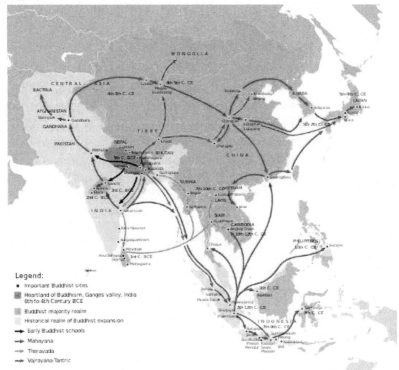

The spread of Buddhism along the Silk Road.
Gunawan Kartapranata, CC BY-SA 3.0 <https://creativecommons.org/licenses/by-sa/3.0>, via Wikimedia Commons; https://commons.wikimedia.org/wiki/File:Buddhist_Expansion.svg

Hinduism was first introduced to China by Indian merchants in the 2nd century CE. Hindu temples sporadically dotted the areas of the Silk Road in China that bordered India; however, all of these temples have been lost to time and weather.

In the previous chapter, we discussed the amazing caves in Xi'an, China, which are filled with a thousand years of Buddhist artwork. Did you know there were also Hindu figures and icons found amidst the statues and art? In addition, many stupas also contain Hindu-influenced statues.

Buddhism was introduced in the 5th century CE. Buddhism began to decline when the Tang dynasty collapsed, and during the 7th century, it was replaced by Islam, which spread along the Silk Road into the port cities on China's southeastern coast in the 7th century CE by Arab merchants. During the 13th century CE, the Mongols brought more Islamic influences deeper into China. Today, there are an estimated eighteen million Muslim adults in China, and there are ten Muslim ethnic groups.[20]

Iconography, an important feature of both Hinduism and Buddhism, was forbidden in Islam, leading to the destruction of many statues and paintings, leaving stupas abandoned to the sun and sand.

When looking back in time, it is clear that Buddhist art left a permanent impact on central Asian art forms. Hellenized Greek art gave the world the first Buddhist statues. Did you know the first Buddha statues resembled the Greek god Apollo?

Greek style permeated Buddhist art, but the foundation for Buddhist architecture remained firmly Indian in nature. The paintings left behind in caves give us countless clues to life during those one thousand years of history. We can see the physical features of the people who traveled to China from various regions, including some who had blonde or red hair. We can see styles of clothing rise in popularity and then disappear, only to be replaced by clothing from a different prominent culture infiltrating the area. The wealth of knowledge contained in Buddhist art is endless.

---

[20] "Islam in China | Pew Research Center."

https://www.pewresearch.org/religion/2023/08/30/islam/#:~:text=Islam%20was%20brought%20to%20China,Islam%20began%20to%20spread%20inland.

A Long-lasting Effect

There is one remaining long-lasting aspect of religion on the Silk Road that we have not yet discussed. That is cosmopolitanism on the Silk Road. If you think about the people who traveled the Silk Road, including missionaries and religious scholars, you must consider that these people set out hoping to meet other humans with viewpoints different than their own.

Part of the adventure and part of the knowledge to be shared and gained involved encountering people from opposing religions and cultures. This is also part of the practice of diplomacy.

Through Silk Road diplomacy, humankind practiced the art of exchanging gifts, learning about others with an open mind, and receiving new information about cultural ideas. Sometimes, this was received with hostility, but other times, it was accepted peacefully.

If we look at the remaining manuscripts we have that were left behind by Silk Road travelers, they all have something important in common. Many of them were distinctly motivated by religion or used religion as the basis of their diplomatic experiences as they traveled and interacted on the trade routes.

Consider Buddhist travelers. Buddhism dictates that a person is always on a spiritual journey, both on Earth and metaphysically, in order to learn and grow as a person. This worldview undoubtedly defined the way Buddhist travelers interacted with travelers who were different from them. This tolerance paved the way for smoother trade and easier connections between cultures on the Silk Road.

People along the Silk Road Today

Today, the political and moral landscape has been forever changed by the Silk Road. The physical paths have long since faded in some areas, but many oasis cities remain. A few of those cities are Khiva, Bukhara, Samarkand, Konye-Urgench, and Almaty.

These cities all have one main thing in common: they are primarily Islamic cities.

The enduring impact of Islam is still felt in Middle Eastern and central Asian cities. Not only are the majority of people Muslim, but the architecture also consists of minarets and domes in the Persian and Islamic styles; it is almost as if time has stood still for thousands of years.

Khiva, Uzbekistan's inner town, known as Itchan Kala, is a UNESCO World Heritage Site. The old city is filled with ornate mosques and tiled minarets and is considered an essential center of the Islamic faith.

Bukhara, Uzbekistan, is a two-thousand-year-old city that also features mosques, tiled minarets, and madrassas. It is home to the 10th-century Muslim architect Samani, and the city is considered the intellectual center of the Islamic world. The city has been impeccably preserved, even remaining the same when Russian influence threatened to take over the region.

Samarkand, Uzbekistan, is considered one of the oldest inhabited cities in central Asia. It has ornate blue-tiled buildings. According to legend, a cousin of the Prophet Muhammad is buried in the city.

Konye-Urgench, Turkmenistan, was a prominent Silk Road trading hub from the 10th to the 14th century. The people living there today still practice Islam.

It is remarkable to think that the Silk Road first came into existence several millennia ago, yet the architectural, religious, and political influences still remain strong today.

Chapter 8: The Silk Road: Science and Technology

Thus far, we have discussed almost every aspect of the Silk Road except for one thing: science and technology. The Silk Road was, of course, home to the exchange of scholarly ideas, and this included scientific advancements. In fact, once people got together to share their ideas and bridge the gaps between different cultures, religions, languages, and locations, history shows that science and technology began to advance rapidly.

Astronomy

One of the first sciences to emerge as an area of study along the Silk Road was astronomy. People used the skies to determine when was the best time to plant or harvest crops, when to host a yearly festival, or to judge the incoming weather. Ancient people combined astronomy and astrology together, thinking they could use the stars to predict the future as well as the seasons.

In 3000 BCE, the Babylonians of Mesopotamia became the first culture on record to begin officially studying these concepts. It turns out the Babylonians worshiped three main celestial gods. Those were the sun, the moon, and the planet Venus.

Their temples were called ziggurats. They looked like pyramids with stairsteps on their sides, which allowed a worshiper to feel closer to the gods in the sky. Their priests did the only logical thing one could think of when worshiping gods in the sky. They carefully watched the movements of the sun, the moon, and Venus until they were able to accurately predict the movements of these heavenly bodies. By 450 BCE, they were able to use mathematics to determine the locations of the sun, the moon, and the planets in the sky.

Shortly before 370 BCE, the trade route appeared on the scene, and the Babylonians' astronomical advances left the region of present-day Sudan with the Greek astronomer and philosopher Democritus. Democritus paid a visit to Babylon, where he learned about the mathematical calculations for the locations of the stars and planets. He then traveled the trade route through Asia Minor and into Egypt, sharing knowledge as he went.[21]

Another Greek philosopher had visited the Babylonians as well. Thales of Miletus, who lived from 640 to 550 BCE, was able to use the Babylonians' mathematical skills to accurately calculate the eclipse of the sun. He combined these skills with Egyptian knowledge to navigate a ship by looking at the stars.

Meanwhile, in India, the astronomy bug was spreading. The Indians displayed both Greek and Babylonian astronomy skills in their own version of astronomy. They translated technical terms from Greek and created their own astrological chart.

Eventually, Indian scholars took both Buddhism and their own astrological knowledge to China along the Silk Road, where China integrated Indian astrological knowledge with their own discoveries. As we speed right along in history, in the 700s, Indian astronomers brought information about the calculation of eclipses and other important related documents based on Greek and Persian discoveries to the caliph's court in Baghdad, where they were translated into Arabic.[22] Astronomy became a major part of the Islamic Golden Age.

We can clearly follow the path of astronomical knowledge back and forth along the trade routes between societies and see how the information grew over time.

Did you know the New Year celebration was determined by ancient astronomical calculations? It is still celebrated every year on March 21st in

---

[21] https://www.worldhistory.org/Democritus/

[22] https://en.unesco.org/silkroad/sites/default/files/knowledge-bank-article/ways%20of%20scientific%20exchange.pdf

many Silk Road regions today, including Azerbaijan, India, Iran, Kyrgyzstan, Pakistan, Turkey, and Uzbekistan.

The New Year celebration is called Nowruz, with variants of the spelling changing slightly based on country and language. Each country and culture has different traditions they celebrate on this day. In Kyrgyzstan, they practice traditional wrestling. In Iran, tales and legends of the mythical King Jamshid are shared with children, and everyone leaps over fires and streams. Other traditions include tightrope walking, horse racing, and leaving lit candles in doorways.

Every region celebrates with song and dance. There are large sacred meals shared among relatives and neighbors. Hard-boiled eggs are decorated in many countries, and there are plenty of activities for children to enjoy.

The main idea behind the New Year celebration is to foster a spirit of community and bridge the gap between local cultures and neighbors. Families reunite, communities come together, and solidarity is promoted between generations.

Mathematics

A close relative of astronomy is mathematics. They go hand in hand, so naturally, math was promoted and shared along the Silk Road.

The Babylonians and Egyptians were some of the earliest pioneers of mathematics, though the subject did not yet have its name. When the Greeks got a hold of the information, their scholars took off and began developing all sorts of calculations.

Our aforementioned Greek philosopher, Thales of Miletus, was also a merchant and a businessman. He realized that math was an important skill to possess when it came to diplomacy and trade. Thales of Miletus was the founder of the mathematical basis that led to Pythagoras's mathematical breakthrough shortly after.

Greek mathematical knowledge traveled along the Silk Road to the Arabs, where the Islamic Golden Age eventually catapulted math to the next level. Funnily enough, the Arabs were very interested in casting their horoscopes, which inspired them to use geometry in astronomical calculations.

The Silk Road carried mathematical knowledge once again with the Muslims into Spain, where the University of Toledo gathered a massive number of mathematical books. Once the Christians reconquered Spain, they raided the university and ended up adopting the Arabic numeral system as their own. Today, we still use Arabic numerals instead of Roman numerals in our math. But here is a little-known secret. The Arabic numerals actually came from India before they were adopted by the Arabs, thanks to the Silk Road information highway.

Alchemy

Around two thousand years ago, humanity began practicing something called alchemy. This English word is derived from the Arabic term *al kimya*.[23] This was the earliest form of chemistry known to humankind.

You may have heard the legends and stories about ancient alchemists who thought they could find the magic formula to change plain metals into precious gold. While this was a laughable pursuit fraught with errant magic, history shows us that these early scientists did begin to develop the scientific method in their experimentation, which set them on the path to making legitimate discoveries.

Meanwhile, the Chinese were in their corner, trying to use alchemy to find the secret of immortality. During this experimentation, the Chinese made a number of accidental discoveries, including gunpowder! Talk about the opposite of immortality, right? Imagine trying to find something that makes humanity live forever and instead discovering the very substance that would go on to kill millions throughout history.

Knowledge from Chinese experiments gradually filtered down the Silk Road toward the west with Indian and Arab traders.

Gunpowder did not reach the Islamic world or Europe until the 13th century. The first known use of gunpowder in the Arab world was in 1326 when Arab soldiers used gunpowder in an attack against the Moors. After that, word began to spread across Europe. Florence ordered the manufacture of cannons and cannonballs shortly after the Islamic battle with the Moors. By the middle of the 14th century, gunpowder had become a regular feature in European warfare.

The real winners in the study of alchemy were the Islamic scientists. Islamic alchemy was taken very seriously. Muslims combined the use of actual science with magic spells. Muslims also received knowledge about alchemy from Hellenistic Greece. During their conquests, Muslims

---

[23] https://www.encyclopedia.com/philosophy-and-religion/other-religious-beliefs-and-general-terms/miscellaneous-religion/alchemy

gathered knowledge from the Persians and the Indians.

In the end, Muslims amassed a vast wealth of knowledge on alchemy, which led them to practice actual chemistry. They also began exploring knowledge of mineralogy, which is the study of the Earth's minerals.

Their knowledge continued to spread westward as time went on, reaching Spain through Muslim traders.

Medicine

The study of alchemy and chemistry led to the study of medicine. Medical knowledge as we know it today was rudimentary to nonexistent during the earliest days of the Silk Road. Many cultures believed illness to be the work of evil spirits, malevolent gods, or witchcraft because they had no understanding of germ theory, bacteria, or homeostasis.

Indians wrote the *Sushruta Samhita,* which defines Ayurveda, around 700 BCE. This is India's most renowned ancient medical text. It was quite advanced for the time. The Indians were able to perform surgeries, including the removal of cataracts from the eyes. They seemed to have a thorough grasp of the workings of the digestive system and most other systems within the human body. They realized that disease was caused by an imbalance in the body, and they understood that bad things could be driven out of the body with medicinal plants, in addition to maintaining a good balance of physical and spiritual energy in the body.

The Greeks were not nearly as advanced, and they knew it. Alexander the Great asked Indian doctors to travel with his army, and some of them stayed with the army when the soldiers returned home to Greece, bringing their medical knowledge with them.

The Greeks did have several great medical claims to fame, however. You have probably heard of Hippocrates, who was known as the "Father of Medicine" for his careful recordkeeping. He wrote down both what worked and what did not. His studies were passed on to Muslims after a number of years, contributing to the overall building blocks of all branches of the medical field.

Do you think medicine contributed to diplomacy along the Silk Road? There are several ways medical treatments could have contributed to diplomacy. In those days, herbs were often used as a form of medicine. A region's herbs could be given as a diplomatic gift by travelers to foreign lands. A gift of herbs or medical substances packed a double punch. They were difficult to acquire, and they also showed the gift-giver cared about the well-being of the recipient.

Let us not forget about the big picture, too! Scientific knowledge was shared between cultures along the Silk Road in the ultimate diplomatic exchange. The sharing of advanced ideas was more than diplomacy; it was a collaboration for the advancement of humankind.

The Compass and Other Technological Innovations

The Silk Road facilitated quite a few inventions that have had a long-lasting impact on humanity as a whole.

One of those inventions was the compass. First created by the Chinese during the Han dynasty, the compass was initially made of lodestone. That is an ore of iron with natural magnetization so that it automatically orients itself toward the Earth's poles when it is able to turn freely.

Scholars estimate that the Chinese began using the compass for navigation sometime between the 9th and the 11th century.

Later versions of the compass brought more complexity and some improvements; however, the basic compass was born along the Silk Road in China.

Papermaking, as discussed in a previous chapter, was a major technological innovation that rocked the world. It first spread in popularity within China, where they tried to keep their methods a secret. Later, papermaking spread along the Silk Road to the outer edges of Asia and into Europe.

Paper was used to share knowledge efficiently, allowing cultures to write down their religious beliefs and academic discoveries, making them readily shareable. Information could be reliably passed on consistently without the natural changes that occur when information is shared only by word of mouth in the oral tradition.

Papermaking led to the invention of woodblock printing presses during the Tang dynasty. In an imperial degree in 593 CE, the emperor ordered Buddhist images to be printed.

From there, the Chinese printed on textiles and printed Buddhist texts. They used a woodblock printing method to print short texts that people could wear as charms. Eventually, they began printing longer manuscripts as scrolls, some of which were found in the famous Buddhist caves near the city of Dunhuang.

By the year 1000 CE, scrolls were out of fashion, and books with pages were being printed. By the 11th century, the Chinese had invented movable type and cheaper paper, making books easier to print and more accessible to the common person.

The printing of books further aided the spread of knowledge along the Silk Road. Prior to books, people had to spend time writing out information. The reliable printed book was a game changer for scholars. These books could be shared and passed from one traveler to the next, or they could be amassed in a library for scholars to travel to and read.

Today, the ancient tradition of Chinese block printing is carried on by a handful of dedicated artisans in China. It takes a team of half a dozen people to create woodblock prints. The blocks are made from fine-grained pear or jujube wood cut down to two centimeters thick. They are then sanded smooth until they are fully prepared for engraving.

The desired images are brushed onto extremely thin paper and then transferred onto the blocks, where an engraver carves the images into the thin wood. They are carved in a manner that leaves the images raised, not indented, making a stamp. When the images are finally ready, they are brushed with ink and pressed onto paper by hand.

Some other noteworthy inventions on the Silk Road include glassmaking, metallurgy, dyeing textiles, irrigation, and the creation of paper currency.

The Silk Road's legacy shines through in many areas. The Silk Road laid the foundation for modern-day science principles in chemistry and mathematics, including the invention of algebra. Today, books are a standard commodity around the world.

The globalization brought about by the Silk Road set the stage for an interconnected world, one where we practice diplomacy and trade. It also left a lasting chain of connections all across Asia, Europe, and North Africa that affected many areas of life.

Chapter 9: The Silk Legacy

The Silk Road might have dissolved with the ease of modern travel, but its legacy will forever continue shaping cultures and societies across the world.

Religious Legacy

The spread of religion through the Silk Road has been one of its most powerful legacies. It still impacts our world today. Millions of people were introduced to Christianity, Islam, Buddhism, and Hinduism from their travels on the Silk Road. In turn, they took home these new beliefs to their communities, where those beliefs blended with the local culture.

The first one thousand years of the Common Era saw waves of new religions spread from west to east. Buddhism spread out of India through central Asia and across China, leaving behind the impressive Mogao Caves in Dunhuang, China, which are filled with centuries of Buddhist art and architecture.

Stupas have been uncovered by archaeologists all across the Silk Road. A stupa in Myanmar was excavated and found to match the style of a stupa in Amaravathi, located on the eastern coast of India.

Buddhism blended with Hinduism, as evidenced by amazing artwork inside the Ajanta and Ellora caves in India.

Zoroastrianism brought the Silk Road regions the first idea of a monotheistic god, which spread through the Silk Road and laid the foundation for a moral code and struggle against good and evil. This paved the way for Judaism, Christianity, and Islam.

Tradesmen, merchants, and missionaries helped spread religion and new ideas. This gave rise to the many shared cultural influences linking together places and people all along the Silk Road.

We can look at the present day and find hints of the Silk Road still evident today all over the world, not just in the central Asian and Middle Eastern regions.

Nomadic Legacy

In the United States, though the trade route never ran through those lands, we still can see remnants of the Silk Road in people's daily lives. Americans drink tea out of fine china cups, with that tea coming from tea leaves found around the world. Some Americans regularly visit a mosque. Most of the products invented and traded on the Silk Road are still important to people today, such as paper, ceramics, cotton and silk textiles, metalwork, and even glass.

The wealthy among us purchase fine oriental carpets, and even cheaper knock-off carpets have various patterns emulating Turkish or Persian weaves. Think about the history of carpets across the Silk Road. Nomads moved around with their sheep, weaving distinct carpets with wool fibers in the places where they stopped to rest across ancient Iran and central Asia.

Consider the fine Turkmen carpet weavers who are still making carpets today. Their ancestors fled the persecution of the tsars and resettled in Afghanistan, among other places. After the Taliban persecuted them in Afghanistan, they fled to Pakistan. Their history consists of nomadic travelers along the regions of the Silk Road, and the Turkmens still travel to this day, though under different circumstances. There is one constant in their lives: they weave carpets with the same patterns as their ancestors.

The Tibetans tell a similar story of travel. After fleeing Chinese dominion, they moved into Nepal and India, following the ancient trade routes of their ancestors. Now, they are living in a new place, weaving historical patterns into cloth as if nothing has changed in thousands of years.

In southwestern Iran, the Persian carpet weavers of Fars still practice their ancient craft in the present day. The skills are passed down from generation to generation by oral tradition. Men shear the wool from their sheep in the autumn, and women spin it into yarn. While the yarn is being spun, men build traditional carpet looms that look like a horizontal frame on the ground. Colored yarn is tied to a web of wool to create a carpet.

The women do the weaving. The designs are based on their nomadic lives. No weaver ever creates the same design twice; each one is unique. The colors are created using wool yarn and dye. The Fars people create dye with items collected in nature. The blues, reds, whites, and browns of the carpets are produced from lettuce leaf, pomegranate skin, cherry stem, walnut skin, and indigo.

When the carpet is finished, they sew the sides down and then burn away any extra wool. This leaves vivid designs that are then washed clean and dried before the final product is presented for sale.

Today, nomadic people still live in Eurasia and follow a way of life based on the traditions of the Silk Road. They include Siberian reindeer herders, Mongolian horse breeders, Tibetan yak herders, and Turkmen shepherds.

These nomadic people were responsible for significant Silk Road contributions beyond just weaving and carpets. They introduced felted wool to the world, which they used to keep warm and dry. They invented harnesses for horses and livestock, created unique bowed string instruments, and developed sustainable portable housing called yurts.

The Legacy of Silk and Fashion

Silk was, naturally, the most well-known product of the Silk Road. The Roman obsession with silk vaulted it into luxury item status. Wherever silk went, money and creativity followed. We can witness the same treatment of high fashion items today, some of which are still made from silk.

Today, China has the International Silk Festival to celebrate the fashion and cultivation of silk. This festival includes a themed fashion show. For example, in 2016, the International Silk Festival's fashion show had a theme of four earth elements on what they called High Fashion Night. They featured Exquisite Metal, Charming Wood, Merged Water and Fire, and Comprehensive Element Earth. The show released twenty-eight fashion trends for the 2017 season.

India also has an international silk fair every year, during which vendors from around the world come to sell silk products in one large trade show with up to 150 merchants.

Like the days of the Silk Road, fashion is often divisive and creative. Fashion designers from Japan and central Asia still incorporate silk into their intricate designs. In India, Uzbekistan, and Syria, embroidery is still being sewed by hand onto silk garments.

In China, the silkworm plays a major role in some regions. Local traditions include the Silkworm Flower Festival, which began in 2014 as a revival of the Silk Road's silk heritage. It takes place yearly in the southern Chinese town of Zhenze, which is known as the hometown of the silkworm. The yearly festival is meant to showcase the current silkworm industry and boost tourism in the area.

The local farmers believe the goddess of silkworms is in charge of the silk harvest, and sacrifices are made to her at the festival. Female silkworm farmers dress beautifully with silk and paper flowers. They make harvest offerings to the goddess as part of the festival.

Gastronomic Legacy

Food cooked today in Silk Road regions is considered another part of the cultural heritage of the Silk Road. Today, along the trade routes, each culture has its own unique flavors and traditions, yet somehow, all of the places still retain links to each other left over from thousands of years of interconnected trade.

In Iran, you will find freshly cooked flatbreads being sold at markets from wooden carts. The breads are flavored with familiar herbs and spices, such as onion, garlic, sesame, and cumin. Travel along the old trade routes to India, Pakistan, Afghanistan, and other parts of central Asia, and what will you find? The same flatbread with different local names and different spices added to it, giving each region a unique flavor.

Familiar fruits and vegetables fill market stalls in these countries as well. You will find fresh persimmons, pomegranates, figs, peaches, grapes, leeks, ginger, and onions. Each region makes slightly different recipes with the same main ingredients.

Another common culinary bond between regions of the Silk Road is the love for dumplings or bread with fillings. China has the mantou, Japan refers to this sweetened filled bread as manju, and in Korea, it is mandu, which is a ravioli-type dumpling filled with beef. Tibetans have filled dumplings called momo. Turkey, Armenia, and Iran have wonton-style pasta with meat, cheese, and/or vegetables as well.

Musical Legacy

Music on the Silk Road has had a major impact on cultures. The world's music is astonishingly diverse, though the most foundational instruments are similar. The human voice, instruments made from natural wood with strings added, flute-style instruments that produce sounds by blowing, and drum-style instruments that produce sound by banging on a hollow object are the most common.

The use of music is similar across all cultures as well, being used for both pleasure and as a part of traditions.

How did music on the Silk Road spread and change over time?

The people on the Silk Road can characteristically be divided into two separate groups: nomads and sedentary peoples. One thing both groups have in common, even if there were multiple conflicts between them, is their music.

When travelers journeyed along the Silk Road, they might have hosted some of the world's first international jam sessions. Imagine nighttime around a fire in a remote Hindu Kush valley or in a cold, desolate desert. Music was a welcome distraction for weary travelers, providing both entertainment and comfort.

Many instruments played by nomadic people along the Silk Road reached Europe rather quickly. This includes lutes, oboes, drums, and zithers. The first violin was likely based on a Mongolian instrument made with horsehair strings. This instrument was held upright and played with horsehair bows. The scroll at the top of the modern morin khuur stringed instrument today is a carved horse's head based on the original Mongol version.

The history of the fiddle can be traced through East Asia and seen in the kamancheh instrument. Indonesia undoubtedly experienced the stringed instrument during the spice trade, fashioning their own version called the rebab.

Nomadic people had a tradition of the bard, a musician who recited poetry or sang in a storytelling style accompanied by music they made themselves, such as a drum beat to represent horse hooves. In communities that are now sedentary, the musical style of the bard still persists today, revealing clues about their nomadic ancestry.

Other musical ties bound the different religions and cultures along the Silk Road, and these are still clearly present in cultural music today. For example, the Buddhists introduced monastic chanting to the world. Present-day Christian Assyrian choirs still sing in monastic chanting, matching the same style of scales and melodic modes of the Middle Eastern Islamic world. Armenia, which is home to one of the Middle East's oldest Christian cultures, and Jewish cantillation both display similar styles of chanting and modal tones.

Today, the music of the Silk Road is still being made. However, the people are far more scattered. Music of the Silk Road remains a link between communities, especially those that have been scattered by immigration or wars. Afghan musicians compose new songs even though they may be living in New York City, Toronto, or Peshawar. Bukharan Jewish music has almost been eradicated from Bukhara, but it is alive and well within expatriate communities in Tel Aviv and New York.

Today, the Aga Khan Music Programme in central Asia collaborates with the Smithsonian Institute and the Silk Road Project to keep the musical traditions of the central Asian portion of the Silk Road alive and thriving in the face of wars, famine, and political upheaval. They currently have projects in Kazakhstan, Kyrgyzstan, Tajikistan, Uzbekistan, and Afghanistan.

Famous cellist Yo-Yo Ma is a well-spoken artist who promotes musical and cultural exchange between present-day Silk Road regions. Born in Paris to Chinese parents before immigrating to the US as a child, Yo-Yo Ma has experienced his fair share of migration. His father was a violinist who focused on bridging the gap between China and the West with music.

Yo-Yo Ma summed up the present-day preservation of Silk Road cultures perfectly when he said, "As a crucible for cultural intermingling, the lands of the Silk Road, then and now, offer an unparalleled vantage point from which to understand vitally alive and ever-evolving languages of music, art, and craft that may seem by turns familiar and exotic. Our challenge is to embrace the wondrous diversity of artistic expression while remaining mindful of the common humanity that links us all."[24]

Today, work is being done by organizations like UNESCO to preserve the intangible cultural heritage of the Silk Road. UNESCO stands for the United Nations Educational, Scientific and Cultural Organization. Their goal is to "promote knowledge sharing and the free flow of ideas to accelerate mutual understanding and a more perfect knowledge of each other's lives."[25]

They define intangible cultural heritage as "traditions or living expressions inherited from our ancestors and passed on to our

---

[24] "A Journey of Discovery | Smithsonian Folklife Festival"
https://festival.si.edu/2002/the-silk-road/a-journey-of-discovery/smithsonian
[25] "UNESCO in Brief." https://www.unesco.org/en/brief

descendants, such as oral traditions, performing arts, social practices, rituals, festive events, knowledge and practices concerning nature and the universe or the knowledge and skills to produce traditional crafts."[26]

UNESCO works to provide in-depth and culturally relevant information on different subjects related to the Silk Road to promote understanding and keep traditions alive. It is a fabulous resource for all things related to the Silk Road.

While we have collections of artifacts that survived the years and give us fascinating clues to study about life during the time of the Silk Road, the real jewels are the intangible cultural heritage still present today in descendants of people who lived along the Silk Road. However, as our world becomes increasingly globalized, these pockets of traditional cultures are at risk of being lost forever.

The Belt and Road Initiative

Did you know there is a collective effort to bring back the Silk Road?

China is working to revive the Silk Road as a new initiative known as the Belt and Road Initiative (BRI). Its goal is to enhance connectivity through trade, boost economies, and grow diplomacy through Asia, Europe, and Africa.

The BRI was first announced by China's president, Xi Jinping, in 2013. The inspiration and name were based on the original Silk Road trade routes. Similar to the original Silk Road, the intentions are to foster connections and exchange cultural information along with trade.

What does Belt and Road mean? The two main components of the BRI are the "Silk Road Economic Belt" and the "21ˢᵗ Century Maritime Silk Road." The Belt portion will focus on the overland routes connecting China to Europe through central Asia and the Middle East, similar to the original Silk Road's overland routes. The maritime routes will connect China to Southeast Asia, Africa, and Europe.

In order to pull off the BRI, a large amount of infrastructure has to be developed, and countries must cooperate with each other to sync up in trade. On the list of infrastructure to be developed are roads, railways, ports, airports, and even pipelines. Energy infrastructure will also need to be in place to power the boats, trains, and trucks traveling along the BRI.

---

[26] "Intangible Cultural Heritage." https://en.unesco.org/silkroad/silk-road-themes/intangible-cultural-heritage.

Funding for the BRI is coming from Chinese state-owned enterprises, companies, banks, and other institutions. Foreign investors have started joining in as more countries decide to join the BRI. China even established a new bank to support the project. It is called the Asian Infrastructure Investment Bank (AIIB), and it is linked to something called the Silk Road Fund.

The BRI has already gathered investors and interest from countries in Asia, Europe, Africa, and even Latin America. Recent projects include the China-Pakistan Economic Corridor (CPEC), China-Laos Railway, and the Addis Ababa-Djibouti Railway.

Some countries have worried about political instability caused by the BRI. Will China gain influence and soft power over countries where it promotes trade routes? Looking back at China's history in the original Silk Road, we may be able to guess the answer to that question.

As of recently, the BRI is still expanding. It now includes digital trade initiatives. When people began to worry about the impact of all of the new infrastructure on the ecosystem, China added a green initiative to the BRI.

China would like to add the BRI to the United Nations Sustainable Development Goals. Countries around the world are watching the beginnings of the BRI, and the debate over the pros and cons continues.

Conclusion

The Silk Road was a vast network of trade routes that connected the Far East to the West in the ancient world. It spanned a distance of nearly four thousand miles (over six thousand kilometers) of territory in its entirety.

The origins of the Silk Road began in ancient China around the 2nd century BCE during the Han dynasty. As the centuries went by, the Silk Road witnessed the rise and fall of empires as it expanded and grew. Eventually, the Silk Road extended as far west as the Mediterranean Sea, incorporating trade with the Greeks, Romans, and many other civilizations.

This trade route brought commerce to remote valleys and crossed dangerous deserts and mountains. The Silk Road was also a maritime route later in its history, fostering the iconic spice trade through the oceans and across the globe.

The sea routes began to take preference over the long, treacherous overland routes as navigation technology improved. The sea routes allowed goods to be transported faster and in larger quantities. Maritime markets also increased access to remote locations and allowed isolated societies to participate in trade.

Maritime routes also allowed for direct trips from port to port, giving rise to port cities all along the waterways. These port cities became melting pots of cultures where scholars and religious leaders met with each other to exchange knowledge and ideas. The societies at these ports were greatly enriched by the diverse cultures in their cities.

Maritime trade routes really increased the speed of globalization by connecting the world efficiently and spreading ideas and religion even further than the land routes had done.

We have seen what an impact the Silk Road had on world history. Take a moment and imagine what the world today would be like if the Silk Road had never even existed. Imagine, way back during the Han dynasty, if the emperor had not felt motivated enough to send out a diplomat to explore nearby regions and establish friendly trade.

What all would have been impacted?

Primarily, we can be certain that the world would have developed new ideas at a much slower pace. For example, ideas and technology that made their way to Europe from the Silk Road would have had to find their way abroad by chance rather than by being carried swiftly along with trade goods on a regular basis.

How long would it have taken for the discovery of gunpowder to make its way to the West? After the Europeans were given information about gunpowder, they rushed to develop firearms. This would never have happened without the Silk Road. How would that have had an effect on the success or failure of subsequent wars? How would that have impacted the expansion of territory or the acquisition of natural resources? And how would that have impacted civilians caught in the midst of warfare?

Christopher Columbus discovered some of the islands in the Caribbean while searching for a maritime route to engage in the spice trade. If there was not a Silk Road, would the rush to discover spices have ever occurred? How long would it have taken for the Americas to be discovered and settled by Europeans?

Imagine the long-lasting impact of that. What would the Americas look like today if they had not been discovered by outsiders at that point in time? More than likely, there would be more native peoples in the Americas today. The landscape of the world would also look like a very different place.

Chances are the continents would have been eventually discovered by sailors from Europe at some point in time, but it could have been hundreds or even thousands of years into the future. Medicine may have developed to the point where Europeans could aid native communities suffering from European diseases like smallpox. However, it is hard to know for sure in this hypothetical universe where the Silk Road never existed.

Human migration would have slowed to a halt, leaving communities more isolated from each other. Without the sharing of ideas through trade, communities would have stayed more homogenous, with cultures and religions staying stagnant due to the lack of influence of other people groups.

Think about the Black Death. This horrific disease spread from trade with the Far East into European cities, where it wiped out large amounts of the population. In some cities, more than half of the population died from the plague. Without trade on the Silk Road, diseases like the bubonic plague would have never spread across Europe. Chances are something else may have wiped out the population in place of the plague, but it possibly might not have done so on the same disastrous scale as the plague.

Europe would have lacked many goods and food items that have become commonplace. Imagine the British people without a cuppa tea! We could write an entire book alone on the importance of tea in British culture throughout history.

The Silk Road also contributed to the loss of indigenous beliefs from nomadic and isolated cultures. Without the spread of religion along the Silk Road, these isolated peoples would have held onto their native beliefs for a longer period of time.

Religion on the Silk Road heavily impacted architecture and art, blending cultures and religions together to create all types of unique buildings and artwork. For example, remember the spread of the blue-tiled mosques with minarets across central Asia? This would not have happened without interconnected travel on the trade routes. Art and architecture would have been isolated to their own regions instead of being influenced by other places.

Missionaries would not have been able to travel from place to place as easily since the Silk Road was heavily used as a missionary route. This would have greatly impacted Christianity, which was spread in large numbers by traveling missionaries.

Without a doubt, the Silk Road was the catalyst that caused economic success in many regions, raising empires to great heights and, in turn, leading to their demise when wars and disasters ended or changed trade patterns.

Think of the Roman Empire without silk. What would the Romans have spent their money on if they had not funneled so much of it into

China? The absence of luxurious silk would have led to an obsession with a different luxury good that was more local to Rome. What might it have been?

The Romans' style would certainly have been different as well. Without silk, the elite would have had to dress in ordinary wool and linen. Without silk, would the Romans have concentrated on developing their own fancy textiles? While the people of the empire loved silk, they still would have traded other goods and flourished without it. They just may have looked less suave while doing so!

Aside from all of the obvious things we would miss without the trade of goods on the Silk Road, perhaps the largest impact would have been the lack of globalization and diplomacy between cultures.

Without globalization, the world would lack economic growth. People would have no access to a wide range of goods from outside of their home regions. Countries would strive to be economically independent without trade, localizing their industries and focusing on producing goods that lay in their backyards rather than sourcing materials from all around the world, similar to the way nomads weave carpets from resources close to home.

The greatest gift of the Silk Road is the human connection it fostered between unique groups of people. The richness and depth humanity as a whole has gained from the sharing of music, art, food, and knowledge can never be replicated.

The Silk Road represents the human spirit of adventure, showing the unending desire we possess to connect with others across vast distances and over challenging terrain. The Silk Road shows how determined humans are to find prosperity, even in the face of dangerous sea voyages or when faced with the steep Hindu Kush mountain range.

Without the unbreakable threads linking civilizations along the Silk Road, we would be isolated, likely remaining in hostile pockets of civilization and lacking the most wonderful parts of what it means to enjoy life to the fullest: the shared connections between people.

Part 2: The Black Death

An Enthralling Overview of a Major Event in the Middle Ages

Introduction

As the world begins to emerge from the recent pandemic, many might struggle to imagine a more deadly disease. However, back in the 1300s, a pandemic known as the Black Death began spreading throughout Asia, Europe, and North Africa, and for many, contraction was fatal. While official death tolls are unknown, some estimations go as high as two hundred million lives lost.

This book will cover what is known about the origins of the Black Death, as well as how it spread across several continents. We will then talk about how the Black Death still affects us today and how the world has adapted to it. Because, yes, this deadly disease is still out there! But keep reading because there's some good news along with all the bad.

Join us then as we journey back over seven hundred years ago to a period full of danger and a fight for survival. Discover the enduring human spirit in the most trying of times. It will not be an easy historical period to examine, but it will be well worth it!

Chapter 1: Origins and Spread of the Black Death

Though understanding about the Black Death was limited at the time of its spread, it is now understood that it was caused by a bacterium (singular form of bacteria) known as *Yersinia pestis* (*Y. pestis*). While the Black Death ravaged Europe in the mid-1300s, it wasn't until 1894 that the specific bacterium that caused the plague was discovered by a physician and bacteriologist by the name of Alexandre Yersin. Originally, the bacterium was known as *Pasteurella pestis* and eventually was renamed after Yersin after his death. While many of you might not be eager to have a deadly bacterium named after you, for many scientists, this is an immense honor!

There was another scientist hard at work to uncover the source of the Black Death at almost the exact same time as Yersin. This researcher was Kitasato Shibasaburo, a Japanese bacteriologist. While Kitasato uncovered the origins, Yersin often gets the credit, as his report was more comprehensive. However, some academics give both men credit for the discovery. Because of their hard work, we are able to understand how this deadly disease is spread.

Y. pestis is a rod-shaped bacterium. When a virus enters our bodies, the first thing our immune system does is send our defense cells, also known as macrophages, to get rid of the intruder. However, the toxins in *Y. pestis* are so aggressive that it does not take long before our defense cells are defeated, allowing the bacterium to multiply with abandon.

Now, before we get into how the Black Death can pass so quickly between people, let's dive into a few of the terms that you will see a lot of in this book.

The two most common are the Black Death and the bubonic plague or, for our purposes, just plague. These both refer to the same disease, but bubonic plague is a bit more scientific. While we'll get further into detail on the specific symptoms in the next chapter, what you need to know is that bubonic refers to swollen lymph nodes. These are most commonly found in the neck, armpit, and groin areas.

A plague refers to a bacterial disease with severe symptoms, such as fever and a chest infection. There are three types of plague: bubonic, septicemic, and pneumonic. In this case, the Black Death generally began as a bubonic plague that then morphed into one or both of the other types of plague.

The term Black Death started being used after observing the way many peoples' skins turned black as their infection worsened.

Black Death and bubonic plague will both be used over the course of this book. Other names that have been used through time include the Blue Sickness, the Pestilence, and the Great Mortality. We likely won't use any of those names, but it's always interesting to see how names change over time.

While many people quote rats as the spreader of this violent disease, after much study, it was determined that something even smaller was to blame: fleas. These tiny creatures became infected with *Y. pestis* and would go on to infect bigger creatures, such as rats, mice, squirrels, and rabbits, through bites. But how would the virus then pass on to humans?

Unfortunately, bubonic plague is incredibly contagious and can spread in almost every way imaginable. Before a virus passes from an animal to a human, there is typically something that happens called an epizootic. An epizootic is basically an outbreak of a disease similar to a pandemic or epidemic for humans, except it's happening within an animal population. An example of an epizootic is bovine spongiform encephalopathy, more commonly known as mad cow disease. Almost 200,000 cows have died of the disease, along with 150 people.

In the case of mad cow disease, the humans who contracted it did so through eating meat from an infected cow, but there are many other ways for viruses to spread.

In the case of the Black Death, once smaller animals died, many fleas infected with the plague searched for bigger prey. Because rats are so common in bigger cities, it was natural for humans to be the next choice. However, it wasn't just flea bites that could pass on the disease. Because the virus is present in blood and other bodily fluids, many people caught it simply from handling diseased animals. For example, someone might have prepared and eaten a diseased animal before it was showing symptoms. Or a beloved pet might have killed a rodent and then passed the disease onto its owner. It might seem obvious to stay away from someone who is clearly sick, but by the time symptoms were present, it might have been too late. Besides, many people at the time had no idea how the virus was spreading, so it's understandable why proper precautions weren't always taken.

The exact origins of the Black Death aren't known, but it is generally agreed that it originated somewhere in central Asia. In the mid- to late 1330s, there was a settlement near Issyk-Kul Lake, which is a mountain lake that is now part of modern-day Kyrgyzstan. The settlement was full of traders, a profession that you will soon understand had a key role in the rapid spread of the disease.

A map of how the disease spread from 1346 to 1353.

How and where the disease spread for the next several years is unknown, but it eventually made its way to Feodosiya, then known as Kaffa, which lies on the Crimean Peninsula in Ukraine. It is generally thought that it was brought there by Mongolian traders.

Wherever it originated from, what we do know for sure is that it was able to spread so quickly because of the trading routes that stretched across Asia and Europe. While it has not been confirmed, it has been suggested that Mongolian warriors catapulted infected bodies into the town of Feodosiya in an attempt to bring down their enemies. Quite a vivid image if it happened!

However, even without catapulting bodies, the Black Death still paints horrific images to think about now. From Feodosiya, several ships set sail for Mediterranean ports. At this period in time, the Silk Road was at the height of its operation. Trading routes crisscrossed their way across Asia, Europe, and North Africa, covering around four thousand miles of land and sea. It's not hard to imagine how a network of paths like this might spread a deadly disease.

In 1347, several ships pulled into the port of Sicily. There were other ports that plague ships pulled into around this time, including ports in France, Spain, Britain, and Ireland, but Sicily is one of the most well-documented cases. What Sicilians discovered when they boarded the ships was horrifying.

Many of the sailors were already dead, and those who were still alive were very ill. It was immediately decided that the ships should be sent back out to sea, but unfortunately, it was already too late. The Black Death had arrived in Sicily, and it soon began to spread inland.

As we'll discuss in the next chapter, the incubation period for the Black Death can be lengthy, so many people were contagious for several days without even knowing it. Because of this, people traveled along roads and into different ports, spreading it to dozens of people, who then went on to infect hundreds of cities with incredible speed. And, of course, communication between different areas at this time was slow, so sometimes by the time a neighboring city caught wind of the fact that the infection was spreading nearby, it had already arrived in their community.

The Black Death continued to decimate populations until 1352 when the worst of the first wave began to decline. This by no means signaled the eradication of the disease, but fatality levels certainly decreased until the second wave during the 1500s.

Of course, there were attempts to limit the spread of the virus, with varying success rates. One of the most common safety measures at the time is a precaution that is still used during outbreaks experienced today: quarantines.

A quarantine is when an individual, a population, or an entire ship is put under lockdown with strict instructions not to leave their designated area. This is done in the hopes that the contagion won't be able to escape the confines of the quarantine, therefore keeping the surrounding community members safe.

It became standard practice to quarantine all ships coming into European harbors for thirty days and then, later, forty days. The Italian word for forty days is *quaranta giorni*, which is where the word quarantine comes from. Why the time period of forty days was chosen is not known exactly, but there are a few theories.

In religious texts, the Great Flood lasted for forty days, Moses fasted for forty days, and after Jesus was resurrected, he spent forty days with his disciples. Forty days could have also had something to do with Hippocrates's theory of illness or even the Pythagorean theory of numbers.

Regardless of why it was chosen, forty days became the standard period of time for sailors to be quarantined in the hope of limiting the spread of the disease.

Populations also learned to be very careful of products that arrived on these boats as well. Fabric, in particular, was suspected to be one of the worst transmitters and would be vigorously washed and aired out for two days before being handled.

During the Black Death, measures now known as social distancing began to be employed. When new ships entered Italian harbors, captains would speak with safety officers through a window in a separate room.

Of course, these measures were implemented differently (it was a different place and time), and many of them were based on guesswork as to how the virus spread. The hypotheses were not always correct.

During this time, plague doctors were a common sight in cities. These doctors would visit people who had a suspected infection and prescribe a quarantine or other safety measure if they were ill. They could also be used as witnesses on wills, which exploded in popularity during this time. These doctors handed out a variety of different medicines, none of which proved to be at all effective. While the disease can be treated with a course of antibiotics today, at the time, no such treatment was available. Instead, doctors would attempt to cure the illness by using rose water on victims or using the popular practice of bloodletting. Bloodletting, which could be done either manually or through the use of leeches, was thought to rid the body of impurities and balance the "humors" within a person's bodily fluids. It is now understood that bloodletting does no such thing.

Stranger than bloodletting was the outfit that later plague doctors wore. Although these outfits didn't actually come into vogue until the 16th and 17th centuries, they are so closely associated with the Black Death that they deserve a mention.

An image of a plague doctor.
https://commons.wikimedia.org/wiki/File:Paul_F%C3%BCrst,_Der_Doctor_Schnabel_von_Rom_(coloured_version).png

The outfit consisted of long pants that connected to large boots. A shirt would be tucked into the pants, and a coat with a protective coating of scented wax would be worn. Plague doctors also had a hat and gloves that were typically constructed out of goat leather, as well as a cane they could use to poke suspected plague victims.

However, the most astonishing feature of this uniform was the mask. Not only did plague doctors put on glasses, but they also wore large bird-like masks that gave them a sinister appearance. The long beaks featured two small holes for breathing.

While it is now known that the plague can spread through droplets transmitted through the air, at the time, most doctors believed that it was due to the aforementioned imbalance of humors. Therefore, it was thought that the right concoction of flowers and herbs could prevent the spread of the disease into the nostrils. Because of this, doctors would fill their masks with herbs and perfumes, falsely believing that the scent would prevent the inhalation of poisoned air.

While the addition of perfume and open breathing holes clearly didn't prevent the spread of disease, there was some wisdom in the original design of this outfit. Medical professionals working with infectious diseases often do so in disposable medical garb that doesn't allow for any skin or orifice to be exposed to outside air. In some cases, full hazmat suits might even be worn. Of course, we now know that face masks that completely cover the mouth and nose are one of the most effective tools we have against airborne viruses, so perhaps it would be pleasing to some of the plague doctors from the past to know that their outfit design wasn't totally pointless.

Vicary Method

One rather bizarre method used to attempt to cure the Black Death was something invented by a man named Thomas Vicary, and it's certainly not for the faint of heart. Although introduced during a later outbreak of the bubonic plague in the 16th century, this method is indicative of the lengths people went to in order to combat this deadly disease. The Vicary Method was employed by plucking all the feathers off of a chicken's backside. That's right; a bare chicken's bum was an essential part of this so-called cure. The bare chicken bottom would then be strapped onto one of the boils on a patient's body. Oh, and it's important to mention that this would all be done while the chicken was still alive!

The idea was that the chicken would breathe in the infection through their bottom because, at the time, it was believed that chickens breathed through that area of their bodies. It might seem ridiculous now, but when you think about the fact that these people were dealing with a disease that was killing millions at a rapid rate, you can't really blame them for trying anything they thought might help.

Once the chicken got sick, it would be removed, cleaned, and then reattached. Obviously, this method didn't succeed in doing anything other than humiliating and infecting a chicken!

Another attempt to curb the spread was the use of plague hospitals. These hospitals sprang up all over Europe and were used as isolation centers for the sick. While not all of these hospitals were pleasant, for many, it was an attempt to allow dignity to those in their final stretch of life while simultaneously protecting the lives of the community members around them.

Unfortunately, attempts to limit the spread were not particularly successful. This was partly due to the limited understanding of how the disease spread but also because it was hard to enforce some of the restrictions. People would flee quarantined areas in the hope of escaping the virus, only to unknowingly take it to another community.

Several cities began implementing death penalties for anyone who tried to cross in or out of a quarantine zone without permission. Traders were looked down on with particular disdain and were often forbidden from entering cities on their trade routes.

Antisemitism and the Black Death

Antisemitism was already rampant throughout Christian communities in Europe for decades before the Black Death took hold. There had been many cases of Jewish communities being murdered across the continent. However, there are some accounts that recall how Jewish communities were falsely accused of having been the ones responsible for the plague outbreak. This completely unsubstantiated claim resulted in massacres of Jewish communities in areas like Germany and Spain. While historians differ on the exact details, pandemics often see certain communities face horrific persecution. If someone wants to attack a specific group, they need very little fuel for their fire.

While there have been several pandemics throughout history, none have been as damaging as the Black Death, and that is in large part due to the speed at which it spread. It is estimated that the virus covered anywhere from 1.5 to 6 kilometers (less than a mile to almost 4 miles) a day. This is even more incredible when you consider the limited speed of transportation in those days.

By the end of the first wave of the plague, it had wiped out almost a third and possibly even up to two-thirds of Europe's population. In some cities, almost 90 percent of the citizens died. The elderly and the immunocompromised were particularly vulnerable to the virus's attack.

The survivors of the first round of the plague might provide a clue as to why the outcomes of the next waves weren't as severe. Although the Black Death continued to see waves for the next five hundred years, the death counts generally weren't as high. This is possibly due to the fact that the ancestors of the next group of people affected by the pandemic were the ones who were able to survive the first wave. This chilling display of natural selection perhaps passed down the ability to be able to withstand the virus, which might explain the lower death counts in the years that followed.

However, even with this slight advantage, the death tolls from the Black Death were staggering. During the summer of 1665, the plague took hold in London, England. During May, only forty-three people died, but by the end of the summer, the virus had killed 15 percent of the city's population. If that level of devastation was possible in just one city during a less severe wave of the pandemic, you can imagine how bad it must have been overall. In fact, after the first wave, it took almost two hundred years for western Europe to reach the same population level that it had had prior to the pandemic.

An illustration of the plague in London in 1665.
https://commons.wikimedia.org/wiki/File:Great_plague_of_london-1665.jpg

Chapter 2: Symptoms and Progression

The incubation period for the bubonic plague is generally four to seven days. However, symptoms can present in as little as twenty-four hours after exposure and can also sometimes wait to present after the week mark. This unpredictable time period would have made it very difficult for people to know who was infected.

During the incubation phase, *Y. pestis* attacks the immune system, but the body is attempting to put up a defense, so there are no obvious signs of the disease at this stage.

One of the most frightening aspects of the plague is how quickly symptoms can appear. Someone might appear to be in perfectly good health and then the next moment be deathly ill.

Fever

People experiencing the Black Death often came down with an extremely high fever that seemed to come out of nowhere. Fevers were often accompanied by severe chills that were almost impossible to manage.

Fatigue

The sudden onset of extreme fatigue was another indicator that the Black Death might be on its way. In the mid-1300s, many people worked as laborers and were used to long, strenuous days. However, the overwhelming tiredness that hit them as a result of the plague left them unable to leave their beds.

Weakness

The plague had the power to take someone from Olympian-level strength to a wave of exhaustion from simply lifting a finger.

Headache

A pounding headache would often overwhelm victims of the plague.

Light Sensitivity

People infected with the Black Death often complained about the harshness of light.

Unusual Tongue Appearance

People who were developing bubonic plague symptoms often had a white or swollen tongue just before their lymph nodes began to swell.

Muscle Aches

While nobody who contracted the plague was in any position to do any exercise, their entire body felt like they had just been put through the most punishing workout imaginable.

Swollen Lymph Nodes

The most distinguishing feature of the Black Death was swollen lymph nodes. Lymph nodes are filters that run throughout our bodies to help drain waste products from our system. They also contain cells called lymphocytes that can destroy harmful bacteria. When our lymph nodes are trying to fight off an infection, they often become swollen. When swollen, the lymph node is referred to as a bubo, which is how the bubonic plague gets its name.

We have lymph nodes in various areas of our bodies, but the areas that are most visible to produce lumps are our neck, armpits, and groin. Not only will these buboes swell to an uncomfortable size, but they can also swell to the point where they need to release some pressure and can actually start to leak pus and sometimes even blood.

These are often the first symptoms that people infected with the Black Death experienced, but each infection was different. Some people would immediately exhibit more serious symptoms. Because no treatments existed at the time, almost everyone ended up exhibiting those symptoms eventually.

There are three different types of plague. While we mainly use the term bubonic plague in this book, the other types, septicemic and pneumonic, can and often do result from an initial bubonic infection. Most of the time, if one does not receive treatment, that is exactly what would happen.

Septicemic plague is the reason why this pandemic was so often referred to as the Black Death. When a patient reached this stage, it was because the *Y. pestis* had multiplied to such an extent that it was beginning to completely take over the body.

Patients with septicemic plague might have started in the bubonic phase or skipped immediately to this much more serious version of the plague. At this stage, the body begins to shut down, which results in gangrene, which stops the normal flow of blood in your body, particularly to areas like your fingers and toes. This kills off skin and tissue, resulting in a black, almost charred look that presents in patches. Once blood flow has been disrupted and the tissue has died, there is no reviving it. While modern medicine can prevent septicemic plague from progressing, without it, the infection will likely kill you within forty-eight hours. The only way to stop the spread without treatment is by amputating the infected areas.

As if that wasn't bad enough, this stage usually comes with severe gastrointestinal symptoms, including nausea, violent vomiting, and diarrhea.

Following the fever you get in the initial stages of septicemic plague, your body will go into a stage known as sepsis. While dead and blackened tissue is the external evidence of this condition, something even worse is happening on the inside. Your body is working so hard to fight off the attack that it creates an internal inflammatory response. This doesn't just disrupt blood flow to the skin; it also affects the blood flow to all your other organs, like your kidney, your heart, and your brain. Even in modern times, sepsis can easily be fatal or cause lifelong medical issues. During the Middle Ages, no treatment was available, so the mortality rate was very high.

Septicemic plague is an incredibly serious condition that can frequently have fatal outcomes, but there was another stage that patients could enter known as pneumonic plague. This, maybe shockingly, is the deadliest form of the disease and is the stage where the virus can be spread via droplets. Pneumonic plague is when the virus has spread to the lungs. While all stages of the plague can include the initial symptoms we listed, the following symptoms are more specific to pneumonic plague.

Breathing Issues

People often reported having shortness of breath and a feeling like they couldn't get enough air into their lungs.

Chest Pain

Because blood flow was restricted, the heart had to work harder than it should, which could result in sharp or constant pain in the chest area.

Coughing

The lungs began to fill with fluid, which made it difficult to breathe and also resulted in consistent coughing. This coughing would be loud and painful and could often produce blood or thick mucus.

Delirium

Because the virus took such a terrific toll on the body, many people would end up in a delirious state. It is said that some would end up babbling incoherently in their final moments on earth.

Even if someone didn't immediately have the pneumonic plague, it was generally just a matter of time before they got there—that is if one of the other two stages didn't end their life first. Without treatment, an infected person could go from being seemingly fine to dead in just a matter of days. It was a quick and devastating disease.

Because the onset of symptoms was so quick and the treatments were far from perfect, the Black Death made its way through populations like wildfire. City officials were soon overwhelmed by bodies and began to dispose of victims of the plague in mass graves. Many people who were charged with handling the victims went on to contract the disease themselves.

An 18th-century mass grave filled with plague victims.
https://commons.wikimedia.org/wiki/File:Bubonic_plague_victims-mass_grave_in_Martigues,_France_1720-1721.jpg

The deaths might have been quick, but they were far from painless. The disease quickly took over every area of the body, leaving victims writhing in agony. Because so little was known about the spread and out of a desperate attempt to stop the pandemic from getting worse, many faced the end of their lives alone or stuffed into crowded rooms filled with other sick members of the population.

The plague continued to ravage Asia, North Africa, and Europe until 1352 when it began to diminish. Though it didn't completely disappear, it was quiet enough that many people were able to go about their normal lives without too much fear. However, less than a decade later, it came back for another wave, which lasted for two more years. By 1363, it had died down again, but it came back just a few years later in 1369. You can probably see a pattern emerging here.

The Black Death continued to visit the citizens of the world on and off over the ensuing decades. However, the second large wave didn't happen until the 1500s, when a new strain attacked with renewed vigor. The final big wave of the disease happened in the 1800s. While it is still possible to contract the Black Death today, the final wave saw some major scientific advancements that rendered it relatively harmless if caught quickly enough.

Chapter 3: Medieval Medicinal Struggles

As mentioned earlier, doctors and the general public at the time had interesting ideas about how to treat infectious diseases. But of course, they didn't have access to fancy labs with advanced microscopes and the scientific know-how that we have today. For example, we now accept the germ theory, the idea that specific organisms are responsible for specific diseases. However, during the 1300s, there was no real concept of what germs were or how a disease could be passed from person to person. Instead, the general public believed in something called miasma theory.

Where exactly the miasma theory comes from is unknown, but it was a theory upheld by a Greek physician named Hippocrates. During the first two waves of the Black Death, the idea took hold of communities all over Europe.

The idea behind the miasma theory was that air that smelled foul was the sign of a poisonous substance present. If this poisonous air was breathed in, it could infect the breather. This was why doctors eventually wore the long beak-like masks filled with various perfumes and flowers. They were trying to keep the miasma out! Bacteria wasn't understood, so it was just believed that bad air, in general, was evil and to be avoided if at all possible.

Interestingly, although the miasma theory wasn't exactly correct, it did help facilitate some changes that ended up having a positive impact on health and safety around the world. Because of the miasma theory, sewage and sanitation measures started being implemented in cities and towns. Proper sanitation is a crucial element of a healthy society, but it was implemented for the wrong reasons because of the miasma theory.

In the case of the bubonic plague, many victims of the disease were said to have an unpleasant odor, which was believed to be a dangerous element to others. However, it's unsurprising that anyone in the final stages of the plague would have a bad smell. Their organs were shutting down. They were vomiting and coughing up blood, and they had boils all over their bodies that were oozing pus and blood. The inevitable smell was likely shocking to the nose, but it had nothing to do with spreading the virus.

Similarly, during periods when raw sewage was left in the street, many people got sick due to the contamination of their drinking supply and any accidental contact people had with waste. The smell, while unpleasant, didn't have anything to do with the disease outbreaks.

So, even though incorrect conclusions were drawn about the miasma theory, it did help change some areas of society for the better. Sadly, however, perfume did not stop anyone from contracting the bubonic plague.

Interestingly, there was another concept that was held in high regard during this time period, and it can also be traced back to Greek physicians, including Hippocrates and Galen. The basic concept of the four humors, or humor theory, is the idea that the body contains four different liquids: black bile, yellow bile, blood, and phlegm. The theory was that in order to prevent sickness, a person needed to keep all of these liquids balanced within their body.

Each of the four humors was connected to a particular condition, and there were different requirements for how much of each humor should be present in a person's body. It was also thought that men and women required a different balance.

The belief in the theory of the humors was so strong that during the Renaissance, there was even a specific diet one could follow in an attempt to balance their humors. What was particularly fascinating about humor theory was that the people who believed in it did not recognize diseases as an attack on the body that was coming from an outside source. Instead, it was assumed that any kind of ailment was simply due to an imbalance that could be rectified with some kind of treatment. Because of this, a variety of aggressive purging methods were used. Let's dive into the specifics of the four humors and what was done in an attempt to balance one's body.

Blood

Blood was generally considered the most important humor, which, all things considered, was a fairly good assessment. People who were considered to have an excess of blood were said to have a sanguine temperament. The definition of sanguine is someone who is generally optimistic, especially in dire circumstances. Not a bad quality to have when facing the prospect of a brutal death!

Excess blood was most commonly associated with springtime and was thought to be connected to qualities of wetness and heat.

While humor theory has long ago been debunked, there is still a persistence in thinking that our bodies have these four different temperaments. Because of this, there are specific suggestions for each temperament group. For sanguine or more blood-heavy people, the recommendation is to stay away from heavy foods, such as red meat and too much bread. Instead, it is suggested they eat light, summery foods, as well as lots of vegetables.

Bloodletting, as mentioned earlier, was a popular treatment for many ailments at this time, but it was seen as particularly useful for anyone suspected of having too much blood. There were a variety of ways to draw blood depending on one's preference or, more commonly, one's social class.

Leeching: If you're already squeamish, that's not surprising. Leeching is pretty much exactly what it sounds like. Doctors would apply live leeches to a patient's body and allow them to suck blood from the patient (or, perhaps more appropriately, victim) until it was determined that they had removed enough to balance the humors. Because bloodletting remained popular for so long, owning and distributing leeches became a lucrative profession. It could sometimes be difficult to procure leeches for a reasonable price, so this type of bloodletting was generally reserved for the wealthy. A fun, or perhaps disgusting, fact is that leeches can drink several times their own body weight in blood. Some of them are able to consume up to ten milliliters at a time.

Cupping: Not as common at the time was cupping. Small incisions would be made into the skin, often by several small blades. Then, a small cup would be heated and suctioned onto the skin in an attempt to draw disease away from the body. This was often done directly on top of buboes since they were the most obvious symptoms of illness. Anyone who has received cupping today can probably imagine how uncomfortable that must have been to receive!

Venesection: For those who weren't able to afford leeches, bloodletting by incision was usually the most common method. This involved a small cut made by a thumb lancet or a fleam. A lancet is a small, double-sided blade. A fleam typically had several blades of different sizes, kind of like the blade you might take with you on a camping trip. After the incision was completed, the blood would be collected under the incision point with a dish. The incision would often be made on a vein very close to the crease of the elbow, but that wasn't always the case.

Because so many people fell sick during this period of time and since the general understanding of disease was so limited, the physicians in charge of administering these treatments were incredibly inconsistent. In many cases, they might not have even been physicians at all. Therefore, the amount of blood withdrawn could vary greatly, sometimes leaving the patient incredibly weak and faint.

Yellow Bile

Yellow bile was thought to signify a choleric temperament. This meant someone who was particularly ambitious and aggressive, often lacking in patience. It was closely associated with the summer season.

Interestingly, bloodletting was not only a solution for what was perceived as an excess of blood but also an excess of all the humors in general. It was almost seen as a magic cure-all. This is fascinating since all bloodletting really did was weaken the person who was on the receiving end of it.

There were a variety of other "treatments" used in an attempt to cure the plague and balance the humors, but since they were often used for any perceived imbalances, we'll cover them after talking about the next two humors.

Black Bile

Black bile was thought to be in excess when someone had a melancholy personality. However, it seems difficult to imagine that anyone who was suffering from the bubonic plague would be anything other than melancholy.

Black bile was thought to mean a person had an excess of dryness and coldness within them and was most closely associated with autumn, although sometimes people would associate it with winter instead. It was suggested that a person with a melancholy personality eat more warm, cooked foods and anything that might have a natural laxative effect.

Phlegm

Although the thought of phlegm might not conjure up any appetizing images, someone with a phlegmatic personality type was seen as a person who was actually quite solid and consistent. They were perceived to be hardworking and quick to take accountability. However, that quality was sometimes to their detriment.

Phlegmatic personalities are generally associated with winter, and people with an excess of phlegm are thought to have a lot of moisture and coldness in their bodies. It was suggested that phlegmatics eat flavorful and salty diets with lots of garlic and onions. A popular method for trying to rid people of excess phlegm was to encourage them to vomit.

Speaking of vomit, now that we have covered the prevailing theories of the time, let's go into more detail about some of the outrageous and sometimes frankly disgusting treatments provided to patients. One of the more bizarre treatments happened during one of the later waves of the plague in the 1660s.

Although Isaac Newton is famous for uncovering the laws of motion and light that are still accepted today, it is perhaps reassuring to know that even geniuses have some very bad ideas.

In 2020, a few of Newton's personal notes were sold at auction, and one of them presented an unusual cure for the bubonic plague. Here is what the note said:

"The best is a toad suspended by the legs in a chimney for three days, which at last vomited up earth with various insects in it, on to a dish of yellow wax, and shortly after died. Combining powdered toad with the excretions and serum made into lozenges and worn about the affected area drove away the contagion and drew out the poison."

Interestingly, this lozenge wasn't the only toad remedy that was recommended to help combat the plague! During this same time period, many people took to wearing dried toads around their necks. This was done not because anyone thought toads were a nice fashion accessory but because they believed that the toxins from the toad would help to draw out toxins from the body. As you can probably guess, the toads did no such thing.

However, toads aren't the only remedies people have tried. Let's dive into some of the other interesting attempts people made at ridding their bodies of the Black Death.

1. Vinegar

Vinegar became quite popular during the Black Death and was often used in an attempt to ward off the disease. A popular story circulated that four thieves entered a residence to loot it after its inhabitants died of the plague, but the thieves somehow never got sick themselves. It was said they covered themselves with a vinegar tonic before they entered the home and were able to keep themselves healthy by doing so.

There were several different versions of the four thieves' vinegar tonic, and it is highly likely that each person who made it used a slightly different variation based on what they had on hand. Although the tonic isn't a cure for the plague, there are still some who are curious about the ingredients and make it because they believe it will be of use to them in some way (those who use it today believe it wards off the common cold; no scientific studies have been conducted to prove this).

The following are some of the most common herbs and ingredients you might find. Although the exact benefits of the ingredients weren't known at the time, many of them do, in fact, have some beneficial medicinal qualities.

Cloves – Cloves have a strong and pleasant scent and some antimicrobial benefits.

Garlic – Anyone who has ever experienced a common cold has probably received the advice to eat some garlic. It has been used in medicine for thousands of years and was often added to the four thieves' tonic.

Sage – It helps with inflammation and has antibacterial properties.

Thyme – It might help combat some infections and is rich in antioxidants.

Cinnamon – Another lovely scent, cinnamon has antioxidant and antifungal benefits.

In the book *Aromatherapy*, the French chemist Jean Gattefossé presented a recipe for the tonic:

"Take three pints of strong white wine vinegar, add a handful of each of wormwood, meadowsweet, wild marjoram and sage, fifty cloves, two ounces of campanula roots, two ounces of angelic, rosemary and horehound and three large measures of camphor. Place the mixture in a container for fifteen days, strain and express then bottle. Use by rubbing it on the hands, ears and temples from time to time when approaching a plague victim."

2. Snakes

If you thought the plague treatments ended with chickens, leeches, and toads, then think again! Snakes had been used in some medical treatments prior to the Black Death, so the idea of using them wasn't exactly new. However, how they were used in this context was likely upsetting for the poor people on the receiving end.

At the time, snakes were often seen as evil creatures. They were sneaky and moved in an unusual way, and many of them were poisonous. Because of this, it was thought that the wickedness of the snake could draw out the wickedness of the plague. So, physicians would chop snakes up into pieces and lay them over the patient's buboes. Not exactly a comforting thing to have happen to you when you are moments away from death.

3. Urine Baths and Feces Paste

It turns out there were treatments that were even worse than chopped-up snakes or a raw chicken bum. At the time, it was believed that urine had powerful medicinal properties, and people would sometimes bathe in it and even drink it in the hopes of benefiting from the golden potion.

Scientists have since proven that urine holds no medicinal benefits, at least none that you can't find from a better source. Even so, the rumor that urine is sterile is still a myth that persists today. However, at the time, the demand for urine was sometimes quite high. Just like with leech breeding, sourcing "good" urine was a rather profitable profession for a period during the Middle Ages.

Now, if for some strange reason you didn't want to dunk yourself into a bath of pee, there was another option available to you: a paste made out of human excrement.

Similar to the snake theory, human feces would be rubbed onto a person's boils with the idea that it would draw the illness out. It hardly needs to be said that not only would that not work, but it would also very likely make the person die faster. Plus, it would have smelled disgusting. But again, these were people living in desperate times, so it's understandable that they would have been willing to try anything they thought might help them get better.

4. Onions

After chopped-up snakes and feces, the idea of rubbing onions all over your body might not sound too bad!

Onions were generally used in a similar way to the last few methods, as they would be rubbed against the signature boils produced when experiencing the bubonic plague. Not only was it believed that onions would help draw out the toxins, but it was also thought that onions were a powerful combatant to miasma, which we covered earlier.

5. Unicorns

That's right, it was thought that unicorns were capable of curing the plague. You might be understandably confused, and so were people in the medieval period.

We know that unicorns don't actually exist, so instead, the horns that were used were sourced from narwhals or occasionally from rhinos. Once the horn was collected, it was ground into a powder and mixed with water to be consumed. Of course, this concoction was only available to the very wealthy since unicorns were notoriously hard to capture. Some said they could only be caught by a virgin woman. It seems highly unlikely that any narwals or rhinos were captured by young virgins, but then again, people thought they were drinking the horn of a real unicorn, so they likely believed the story.

6. Flagellation

As has already been stated, there were many who believed the Black Death to be something wicked and evil. And so, it makes sense that many took the plague to be a punishment from God for their sins. In the hopes of paying for their sins, groups of people took to the streets and publicly whipped themselves, often with whips embedded with nails.

Of course, this did nothing except wound people who were likely already sick.

7. Expensive Powder

"Unicorn" powder wasn't the only expensive substance that was mixed into water for people to drink. Another popular potion was the beautiful shiny gem made famous in *The Wonderful Wizard of Oz*: emeralds. Doctors would crush emeralds into a powder and have their patients eat or drink it. Why this was seen as a possible cure is unclear, but then again, that question could be asked about many of the items on this list.

8. Cheap Powders

Of course, the previously listed powders came at a cost and were only available to those who could pay. But it seems that the idea of drinking a powdered drink took hold of the general population, so cheaper and more easily accessible ingredients were substituted for those who weren't able to afford a gem or mythical animal. Both have a long history of being used for various medical conditions, but the reality is that neither of them plays any role in healing a person and could have the opposite effect. Both arsenic and mercury are incredibly toxic and can kill very fast upon consumption. Why they continued to be used after so many people died soon after drinking these potions is a confusing question that has no answer.

9. Theriac

Theriac was a very popular concoction during the Black Death. It was a highly intricate recipe that required dozens of ingredients. It could be used as a paste spread over the skin or was sometimes mixed with a thinner liquid and drunk as a beverage. When made into liquid, it was sometimes called treacle.

While theriac contained many ingredients, including the alarming addition of viper flesh, there is one ingredient in particular that might help to explain its popularity: opium. Opium is a well-known painkiller, and this substance often contained high levels of the drug within its recipe.

Theriac wasn't just a product of the plague; it had also been used by different cultures for centuries, dating all the way back to Mithridates VI, who was alive during the 3rd century BCE.

Out of all the supposed treatments for the Black Death, this is one of the only ones that seemed to provide any actual benefit. However, it is thought that most of that benefit was actually due to the placebo effect. While theriac is still talked about today, there haven't been many studies done on the original recipes, so it's hard to know if it could have helped. However, if nothing else, it probably helped to relieve the pain suffered by plague victims, and it certainly must have smelled better than onions or feces!

10. Fire

Another method people used to try to rid themselves of disease was to sit beside extremely hot fires. It was believed that a person could sweat out a disease if they stayed by a fire long enough or that the heat would destroy infected air. While the thinking behind this wasn't completely accurate, there was definite value to the idea of combating the plague with heat. We'll get to that in more detail in a later chapter.

One particular proponent of the heat method was Pope Clement VI, who was the head of the Catholic Church when the first wave of the plague hit. On the advice of his physicians, the pope spent most of his days in a large room with a roaring fire at either end. He also kept to himself, essentially quarantining inside a room of fire.

For the pope, at least, this method worked, and he died from unrelated causes in 1352.

11. Air

As we talked about earlier, there was a strong belief in the idea of miasma, and many people tried to use that theory to their advantage. It was common to attempt to cleanse the air in one's home by using various herbs and perfumes. Some people would even carry flowers around with them at all times, believing that they wouldn't contract the plague if they were constantly breathing in a pleasant aroma.

Others had the opposite belief and thought that staying near rancid smells would help to draw disease away from them. Because of this, they might stand next to sewage or even decomposing remains, believing that the plague would be overwhelmingly attracted to the bad air and leave their bodies to seek out miasma instead.

12. Quarantine

The only effective method of preventing the spread of the Black Death at the time was quarantining. This obviously did nothing to help people already infected with it, but separating the sick from the healthy did help limit the spread.

Social distancing was another proven method of prevention. However, both quarantining and social distancing were met with disdain by many. It was common to have people purposefully disobey quarantine orders and either move from cities or visit those who were already known to be sick. This resulted in many more people falling ill than if they had followed quarantine and social distancing recommendations.

This disregard for public safety measures has been repeated throughout history. This has often led to extremely strict and sometimes violent lockdowns by local governments. Still, scientists emphasize that quarantining is a very effective and useful measure until the disease in question is under control.

There were undoubtedly countless other treatments used over the years as the Black Death made its way around the world. But these were the ones that were popular enough to still have records of them preserved today. Thankfully, we are much more knowledgeable in modern times, so no one has to strap a chicken to themselves anymore!

Chapter 4: Europe during the Plague

Although the Black Death was present on several continents, it greatly impacted Europe. After its arrival in the 1330s, waves of the disease continued to roll through the continent for hundreds of years, killing millions and leaving many cities altered for generations. Let's look at some of the most dramatic changes that happened during this time.

Conflict

The Black Death had an interesting impact on conflict. Initially, it was so overwhelming that it caused a pause in the conflicts of the day, but that soon reversed in a dramatic fashion, resulting in even more violence than had been experienced previously. During the Hundred Years' War, fighting had to stop completely for a time, as the military was overrun with deaths.

Labor

One of the biggest issues to come out of the Black Death was the loss of workers. One of the most common professions at the time was laborers who worked in agriculture. This was before modern technology greatly reduced the need for physical bodies to tend the land, and workers at the time were an essential element for the production of food and the cultivation of land and animals.

With such significant death tolls, landowners suddenly found themselves without anyone to tend to their farms, and they quickly began to panic. But this was where a small silver lining of the Black Death appeared.

Before the arrival of the bubonic plague, field laborers were seen as some of the lowest members of society. They were peasants who were paid extremely poor wages and were often only making enough to get by. However, the plague changed everything.

Because so many workers died, the landowners no longer had the upper hand, and menial workers could now demand more. With no other choice, they had to provide their workers with good wages or risk losing their profits entirely. The loss of lives also reduced the cost of land, and suddenly, rents cost next to nothing.

This greatly reduced the number of people in the peasant class and gave many people who had survived the plague a better quality of life. And not only did landowners finally have to pay their workers a reasonable wage, but many of them had to actually go to work themselves! While they had previously looked down on many of the jobs on their land, they could no longer afford to be particular. They, too, had to get out in the dirt and get their hands dirty.

However, this idyllic moment of equality was short-lived. Not satisfied with simply paying their employees a living wage, landowners quickly turned to the law to deal with their issues. This issue was particularly fraught in England, where the imposed laws eventually led to a revolt.

In England, a statute was pushed through that followed the details of an ordinance that was passed in 1349. The ordinance stated that anyone under the age of sixty who was not able to work privately was required to work. Not only were they required to work, but they also had to sign contracts that agreed to only pay them wages that had been established prior to the appearance of the Black Death. This meant a swift return to the poverty wages that had been so common prior to the pandemic. It's also important to consider that not only were these wages poor, but they were also being forced upon people who were very likely performing much more work than had previously been required of them. Laborers always had strenuous jobs, but with the loss of so many lives, they had to pick up the slack somehow and were still expected to do so for very low pay.

And it wasn't as though workers could simply refuse to take the work. The ordinance required that they take the first job offered to them, and they could be severely punished if they refused and remained unemployed. This forced workers into a very tight corner and gave power back to the landowners.

This is a common theme during pandemics. A worker shortage happens, and bosses reluctantly pay their workers more, as it is suddenly acknowledged that these so-called "lowly" workers are actually essential. However, once the panic wears off, the people in charge do everything they can to claw back any benefits they give their workers in the hopes of maximizing profits and lining their own pockets.

However, in the case of the Black Death, the renewed power of the landowners didn't last long. The measures lasted for several years, but resentment continued to brew. Under King Richard II, tolerance for these outdated systems finally ran out.

Not only were workers being forced into low-paying jobs, but the king had also implemented a poll tax to help fund military operations, and that was where people's patience snapped. The tax was high and took a large portion of workers' already limited resources.

Eventually, some citizens in England decided not to pay the tax. The king sent out tax collectors to different villages, but they came back empty-handed. In an attempt to keep his power, he decided to send soldiers out in the hopes of collecting the taxes, but again, he was denied. However, the damage had been done, and the peasants had had enough.

On June 2nd, 1381, a group of over sixty thousand people marched to London. They came from communities all over England and were led by a man named Wat Tyler. As they made their way into the capital, they burned down any government buildings and official documents they could get their hands on. They were particularly interested in destroying tax records.

As the crowd entered the streets of London, the mission became a little diluted. Some seemed eager to simply create mayhem, and violence and mischief broke out. However, there were many who still had their initial purpose in mind, and the king eventually agreed to meet with Wat.

The meeting went well. King Richard probably realized he was out of options and agreed to the demands of the workers. The two men made an agreement that the crowd would go home. Unfortunately, some members of the revolt had other plans.

While Wat Tyler and the king were in their meeting, a group went to the Tower of London, where they viciously murdered the archbishop of Canterbury and the treasurer. Upon learning of this, the king was understandably terrified, but he agreed to meet Wat one more time. This time, the meeting was also attended by the same rebels who had committed the murders at the Tower of London, as well as the mayor of London, Sir William Walworth.

Although the king seemed open to hearing the rebels' demands, the mayor quickly grew violent, and he ended up lashing out and stabbing Wat in the neck.

Wat was taken to hospital, where he was assassinated. However, despite the killing, the king did end up agreeing to the new demands, and the rebels dispersed.

While the revolt itself was over, the peasants did not end up getting what they had hoped for. While the king ended up removing the poll tax, he backtracked on all of his other promises, and workers soon found themselves once again forced into low-paying labor jobs.

While the working class didn't gain all the victories they were hoping for, it wasn't a completely unhappy ending for them. Because it took so long for the population to go back to pre-pandemic levels, many landowners were eventually forced into paying higher wages out of necessity. So, even if some of the rebels in the Peasants' Revolt didn't get to enjoy that, at least some of their descendants might have.

Inflation

Just as the world is currently experiencing a spike in inflation, so did people living during and after subsequent waves of the Black Death. It wasn't just landowners who were dealing with a spike in costs because of the pandemic. Everyone felt the squeeze. Trading, which had become fairly commonplace, suddenly became a dangerous occupation. Traveling increased a person's risk for disease, and not only that, but many cities were incredibly strict about letting traders in and out. They might be ostracized or face weeks of isolation just to get the chance to sell their products.

Because of this, the cost of almost everything went up, which meant lots of people struggled to afford the daily necessities.

Art

When people have no hope left or are trying to discern meaning in the midst of an unimaginably difficult experience, they often turn to art. Because the Black Death kept the world in its grip for so long, there were large periods where artists constantly had the thought of the disease in their minds.

Indeed, both the Renaissance and the Baroque periods of artistic expression happened while the bubonic plague was still ravaging the world. It's a great testament to how necessary and important art is, even in the face of death.

Of course, religion was also a very important part of life during this time, and many artists used their art to try to answer questions they had about God or what the afterlife might look like. Some even used their art in an attempt to convert sinners and bring them into the church. After all, many believed that the plague was a punishment for the sins of people, and it was thought that if enough people were good children of God, then the sickness would disappear.

For many artists, their work during this time was highly dominated by images of death. This is a natural response when one is experiencing grief, and art is often used as a way to process the traumatic events one experiences. However, that doesn't make the pieces themselves any less troubling to see.

One such painting is the *Citizens of Tournai Bury Their Dead* by Pierart dou Tielt, a Belgian artist.

Part of Citizens of Tournai Bury Their Dead.
https://commons.wikimedia.org/wiki/File:Burying_Plague_Victims_of_Tournai.jpg

Some depictions of death were morbid, but others were regarded as humorous, at least at the time. This is true of The Triumph of Death with the Dance of Death. This image features several people, as well as skeletons, dancing around the Queen of Death. The queen stands on top of a coffin that contains the pope and the emperor, a reminder that the plague was capable of killing everyone, even the rich and the powerful.

In the painting, the people dancing offer the queen gifts and all manner of riches, but she doesn't want them. All she wants is their lives. While it may seem strange to us now, a wicked queen who could never be satisfied was seen as entertaining. However, it also demonstrates something else. In the image, the living are dancing with the dead, which offers up the idea that even if you're about to die, you should still love and enjoy life while you can.

Another similarly named but far less amusing painting, *The Triumph of Death* by Pieter Bruegel the Elder, depicts the grim realities of the plague. In it, you see a small village that has been completely destroyed by the disease. Dead bodies litter the ground, and all around the village are scenes of fires and abandoned or quarantined ships. While it might seem extreme, that really was what some communities faced. The Black Death killed extremely fast, and sometimes, the bodies would pile up so quickly that the authorities didn't know how to handle it. That was, of course, if anyone in an authoritative position was still alive.

The Triumph of Death.

Although there are several notable artworks that were created during the plague, we'll leave you thinking about one final piece. It's titled *Human Fragility* and was painted by Salvator Rosa in 1656. In it, Rosa paints an image of his child and his mistress. Death is nearby, cowering over his son. It signifies the loss of his child and the shortness of life. One can only imagine what these artists must have been experiencing when they created these works.

While many of the artworks made during the Black Death were certainly depressing, there were also many celebrating the joy of life and how precious and fleeting it is. These works provide a look into the minds of people who experienced these times and what they must have been thinking.

Tombstones created during the Black Death can also offer insights into the artistic expression of the time. While there were many who chose to have peacefully sleeping figures as the sculptures atop their tombs, there were others who chose much more graphic images. Some chose to have their tombs adorned with an image of Death himself. Morbid, yes, but perhaps fitting given the circumstances.

Antisemitism

As was mentioned earlier, the Black Death gave rise to a wave of antisemitism across Europe. Thousands of Jewish people were killed by mob attacks or by barricading Jewish people into buildings or pits and burning them alive. Although many historians have claimed that Jews were slaughtered because people falsely blamed them for being the origin of the Black Death, there are others who contest this idea.

This is because antisemitism was already rampant throughout Europe, and many Christian communities were already eager to rid their towns or villages of those with different religious beliefs. Persecution against the Jewish people had already been happening for centuries, so it's certainly possible that the only reason the Black Death was ever connected with the influx of hate crimes was because it was a convenient excuse. One of the most persistent lies about how the Jewish people were responsible for the Black Death was because they had supposedly poisoned wells, ensuring that the disease would spread through cities via the drinking water. This, aside from being a blatant falsehood, was also a very weak and illogical explanation for the origins of the plague. First of all, where would they have gotten the plague to poison the wells to begin with, and second, why on earth would they poison the very water they themselves had to drink? But, of course, many people don't need logic to fuel their hatred. Just a tiny wisp of a story will do.

While murders of Jews happened all across Europe, the most concentrated massacres happened in Germany, a bleak foreshadowing of the genocide that would happen there hundreds of years later.

An image of Jews being burned during the Black Death.
https://commons.wikimedia.org/wiki/File:Doutielt1.jpg

Many of these attacks were led by Christian governments and churches. Eager to keep control of their communities, they made up terrible lies that Jewish people were plotting against the Christians and, therefore, needed to be disposed of. It was said that Jews were tortured into giving false confessions to crimes they never committed as another way to "justify" the attacks against them.

A term you might commonly hear mentioned when learning about the antisemitic attacks during the Black Death is "pogrom." A pogrom is a word that is Russian in origin. It refers to a violent mob or riot that is created with the express purpose of killing or banishing a particular religious or ethnic group. Pogroms are overwhelmingly enacted against members of the Jewish community.

Of course, the Jewish community fought back, but they were often overpowered. In a famous act of resistance, the Jews in Mainz, Germany, managed to fight back against the mob that was after them. They even managed to kill two hundred of their attackers. However, they were soon overwhelmed. Realizing they were facing a certain death, they chose to lock themselves in their homes and set themselves on fire rather than die at the hands of their attackers. Over six thousand Jewish people died there, and that was just one of many places where they were attacked.

Over the course of the Black Death, Jewish communities, which had had close to four hundred in numbers all over Europe before the pandemic, were reduced by half.

Again, the major correlation between Jews and the Black Death is simply that the Black Death presented antisemitic Christians with a convenient excuse for them to exercise their hatred. It is very likely that there were many people who had a clear understanding that there was no validity to the claim that the Jews were responsible for the Black Death. But many people would have circulated the lie on purpose with the simple desire of fueling the fire and encouraging more people to lash out against the Jewish community.

There were some who attempted to stop the attacks on the Jewish community. Pope Clement VI attempted to point out the irrationality of Jews starting the plague themselves. However, there were many others who encouraged the massacres and others who even managed to profit from it. The Holy Roman Empire agreed to the massacre of Jewish people as long as they received a payoff from the sale of all the personal belongings that were taken from the murdered families.

Religion

While we'll go further into the impact religion had during the Black Death in the next chapter, it's worth mentioning here that religious communities actually lost a little bit of power during this time.

Some people accepted that death was right around the corner and turned to a life of debauchery and excess. They stopped worrying about the societal expectations of the time and instead chose to spend their remaining days enjoying drink and merriment.

There were others who lost their faith in God. As more and more people fell prey to the hands of death, many people questioned their faith and how they could possibly love a God who cared so little for them. Even if the plague was a punishment for their sins, there were some who felt the punishment had gone too far and looked for solace in other forms of spirituality.

This turned a lot of people onto the idea of mysticism and old folk stories as a way of trying to make sense of what was happening around them. While religion still held strong across the world, there was a definite pulling away and a search for deeper meaning during this time.

With such a tremendous loss of and disruption to life, Europe was sent into an unstable condition that lasted for generations. It was a long time before the population stabilized, and it is very likely that anyone who survived the bubonic plague was forever changed. With so many deaths, it is very unlikely that there wasn't anyone alive who didn't have several people who they were close to die. People lost their friends, family, government officials, and religious leaders. Some villages were almost completely wiped out. The full extent of the Black Death's impact cannot possibly be comprehended by those who didn't live through it.

Chapter 5: The Role of Religion in the Age of the Black Death

There were three main religious groups in Europe during the Black Death: Catholics, Muslims, and Jews. Each religion was heavily impacted by the plague and dealt with it in different ways. Let's look first at Catholicism. Now, of course, Catholicism is a branch of Christianity, so we may, at times, use the terms interchangeably. But it is important to note that while all Catholic people are Christian, that doesn't mean the opposite is true. However, the most dominant form of Christianity at the time in Europe was Catholicism, so that is the term that is often used in this book.

Even before the start of the Black Death, the Catholic Church was facing some difficulties. While many might strongly associate the church as having its headquarters in Rome, during the early 1300s, a massive change took place that certainly ruffled feathers in several communities.

The church had been stationed in Rome for quite some time, but in 1309, the political situation there had become volatile. There had already been fractures within the institution itself, but one thing seemed to be clear: staying in Rome wasn't a viable option. Instead, it was decided that the pope at the time, Pope Clement V, would relocate to Avignon, France. This created quite an uproar among Catholic communities, particularly in England and Germany. It was thought that the move to France had damaged the integrity of the church and created a situation where the pope was more invested in the desires of the French monarchy rather than the needs of the faith itself.

The Avignon papacy lasted for quite some time, with seven popes in total residing there, and the trouble it caused cannot be overstated. In fact, it was the move to Avignon that eventually led to the Great Schism (also known as the Papal Schism or Western Schism), which was when three different popes operated at the same time, causing great division for several decades.

The Black Death arrived several years before the schism took place, but it is worth mentioning so you can better understand the kind of tension that was simmering in Europe at the time.

The popes in Avignon were attempting to modernize the church, but the Black Death put a damper on many of their plans. The death tolls were so high, particularly in Rome, that many began to feel resentful toward the church for its decisions.

Catholics were firm in their belief that not only was the Black Death contagious, but it was also a punishment for one's sins. However, Muslims had a different response.

Looking at examples of what was happening in the Middle East, Professor Michael W. Dols wrote that the general feeling was that the Black Death was not a result of one's sins and that the response to it was one of prayer and humility.

Large processions and ceremonies took place, and members of the faith were encouraged to be extra pious. Interestingly, it seemed that Muslims did not support the idea that the plague itself was contagious. They held the belief that the sickness was a gift and would transport the sick to paradise after their death. Because it was thought that each sick person had been chosen by God individually, it was deemed unnecessary to isolate or quarantine a victim. Instead, Muslims were encouraged to remain with the sick.

Sadly, there is little research available on how the Jewish population felt about the Black Death or how they responded to it. Because they were facing such extreme violence, mainly at the hands of Catholics, most of the research that exists is focused on their persecution, not their response to the disease.

For a long time, there was a persistent rumor that Jewish communities suffered fewer deaths from the plague than other communities; however, fact-checking this theory has proved difficult. It has been suggested that this was due to the strict diet and cleanliness standards that Jews were expected to adhere to in their faith, but historians have rightly pointed out that even the most rigorous sanitization standards wouldn't stop fleas or animals from spreading the disease. Instead, it is much more likely that a rumor was started that Jewish people were not as affected by the disease as a way to continue to fuel the idea that they were somehow responsible for the Black Death in the first place.

Now that we've covered the major religions that were active during the Black Death, let's dive deeper into how each group responded to it.

Rise of the Flagellant Movement

While we briefly touched on the flagellant movement earlier in this book, what we didn't cover is that the response wasn't always so extreme.

In fact, Catholics' initial responses to the plague weren't all that different from the Muslims. While their beliefs about why the Black Death had descended upon them were different, both groups doubled down on their commitment to God. Catholics took to the streets and led processions throughout cities and villages. They built shrines to God and the Virgin Mary and prayed continuously.

There were many who believed that certain amulets or charms were capable of keeping them safe, so it wasn't uncommon to see Catholics carrying these items with them.

These processions continued for quite some time, even after it was understood that the disease was contagious and that spending too much time together in groups was dangerous.

However, after several months of peaceful processions, the faithful began to lose faith in their churches. They couldn't understand why God hadn't yet freed them from the clutches of such an insidious disease and became convinced that the church wasn't doing enough. Something more drastic needed to be done. This was when the flagellant movement began to gain traction.

The movement seemed to originate in Austria in 1348 but soon spread to other parts of Europe. Despite the chaotic nature of the group, its members were remarkably organized.

Someone would be appointed leader or "master" of the group, and they would march the other flagellants into different towns, often ending their march at a church. This group would often be several hundred people strong. During the march, they would often wear long cloaks and crosses, but upon arriving at their destination, they would strip off their clothes until they had nothing covering their upper half.

A 15th- or 16th-century woodcut of flagellants.
https://commons.wikimedia.org/wiki/File:Nuremberg_chronicles_-_Flagellants_(CCXVr).jpg

At this point, they would begin chanting and saying fervent prayers while taking out whips that were typically knotted with pieces of metal. They would beat themselves with the whips until they were bloody and eventually fell to their knees. Some groups would then form themselves into the image of a cross on the ground while the master read out a letter calling on other members of the community to repent. It was also common practice for the flagellants to take positions that signified some of the accepted sins, such as murder or adultery.

This whole process would then be repeated in the next town. While you may not think this would be appealing to many, the flagellants managed to build quite a following. The flagellants were angry at what they felt were inadequacies of the church, and this was their form of rebellion. Many people also viewed joining the flagellants as a way to avoid the plague. They felt the church wasn't doing enough, and this was seen as a valid form of prevention or cure. There was also something appealing about the organization. The group was very ritualistic, and in a world that had become increasingly chaotic, something was reassuring about having a routine. It didn't seem to matter that the routine involved brutally beating oneself.

Unfortunately, this group didn't just punish themselves. While they believed that the Black Death was a punishment for their sins, that didn't seem to stop them from blaming other groups for it. The flagellants were instrumental in persecuting the Jewish people and several other groups. They had quite an appetite for blood, and that was very appealing to people who had lots of anger and nowhere else to put it.

At first, the church put up little resistance to the flagellants. While their methods were extreme, they seemed to be giving people purpose and order, and it didn't initially seem like the movement was presenting a challenge to Catholic values.

However, as time went on, the church became increasingly concerned about the popularity of the flagellant movement. It was seen as operating in direct contradiction to what the church stood for, and citizens of various towns and cities often acted in ways that were not approved by the church. People fed and watered the flagellants and invited them into their homes. Sometimes, the bells of local churches were even rung in celebration of the flagellants' arrival, an act that was done against the church's express wishes.

The flagellant movement was unique in that it was accessible to people of all classes. While only the wealthy were able to afford certain treatments, such as leeches or emeralds, anyone who was tired of the Catholic faith could join the flagellants at no cost. The flagellants were people's chance at salvation. And if nothing else, they were seen as excellent entertainment. Just as ancient Rome enjoyed watching gladiators engage in combat, villagers looked forward to the exciting displays of public song, dance, and violence during the Middle Ages.

While the flagellants eventually descended into chaos, at the beginning, they had a set of strict rules that they were all expected to adhere to.

1. No bathing.
2. No interaction with someone of the opposite sex.
3. No changing of their clothes, no matter how bloody or sweaty they ended up.
4. They had to have whipped themselves for eight hours over a certain period of time.

5. They had to pay a certain amount of money toward nourishment each day.

Some groups also planned their processions to match up with the age of Jesus Christ when he was crucified.

Pope Clement VI explicitly condemned the movement. He attempted to stop their attacks on minorities, but support for persecution of the Jewish community and other groups was too strong for his objections to have any impact. However, the church's opposition and eventual expulsion of many of its members was the beginning of the end for the movement. Within a year of the pope publicly denouncing them, their numbers began to fade.

The Black Death wasn't the first time flagellation had gained popularity, and it wasn't the last. But the movement during the plague was likely the biggest of its kind that will ever be seen in history.

Another reason the flagellant movement might have gained the popularity that it did was the lack of access to holy figures. Many priests died or were forced to close the doors to their churches. And traveling to places of worship became difficult in the face of so much chaos. Because of this, worshipers were no longer able to confess their sins to a listening ear and be absolved.

Confession of one's sins is a major element of the Catholic faith, and the loss of this routine was devastating. People started to confess to doctors or friends, people who could not absolve them. And from this issue sprang a thirst for something called indulgences, which brings us to a surprising element of the impact of religion during the Black Death: profit.

It should not be news to hear that some people are happy to profit off of other people's desperation and misery. In fact, tragedy can be an excellent time for people with no morals to make some money.

Indulgences were special documents that forgave people for their sins. They were handed out by the pope and were typically reserved for people who had served the church in some way, such as participating in a crusade. However, due to the unusual circumstances of the Black Death, indulgences became a way for people to receive the relief they had formally only been able to attain at confession.

Anyone with enough funds started purchasing indulgences from traveling sellers. Some indulgences were real, and some were not. Either way, it was a profitable business.

There was also an influx in the selling of religious symbols, such as amulets, which claimed to help protect the wearer from the plague. Whether or not the person selling these so-called protective items was actually part of the church isn't particularly relevant, as they were still taking advantage of poor souls who were doing anything they could to protect themselves.

Even in death, Catholics were willing to pay for the hope of a better afterlife. At the time, it was thought that a Mass held in their name would absolve their sins even if they hadn't been able to achieve that goal while they were still alive. Because of this, it became fashionable to pay to hold Mass after someone's death. This was very lucrative for bad actors willing to take advantage of people and very trying for members of the church who had the best intentions but were then required to perform multiple ceremonies each day.

The search for profit during this period was also present within Muslim communities as well. So many people were dying that gravedigging became a very lucrative profession, so many specifically sought out that line of work. However, not everyone was seeking compensation from the dead. There were also many volunteers at these mass gravesites who seemed to view the work as their responsibility to the dead.

It became common for mosques to hold mass funerals. The death tolls were so high that it was almost impossible to hold funerals for just one individual at a time.

Just as was true of Catholics, some Muslims also turned to mysticism in the hopes of answering some of the impossible questions they had surrounding the plague that had taken over their lives. There were some who believed that the Black Death was not the work of Allah but was instead the result of the evil deity known as Ahriman, or servants of the deity. Because of this, there was also a surge of demand for amulets and special charms that they hoped would protect themselves against this evil.

Religion has played an important role in major crises throughout time. However, the bubonic plague was a true test of many people's faith. For some, it was a comfort, one of the only places where people could feel like they truly had someone looking out for them. For others, it became something that they questioned and eventually lost faith in.

The rise of the flagellants and the brutal persecution of Jewish communities highlighted the darkness that is also present in the most dominant religions in the world. While there were many who sought peace and kindness during such a difficult time, there were many others who purposefully pursued violence and destruction, often hiding behind religion in order to execute their desires.

While many questioned their faith during this time, the desire to be seen favorably by one's God and have a good afterlife seemed to be too tempting for the masses to ignore. While religious institutions certainly had their fair share of difficulties during this time, they also enjoyed enormous profits and support. As is still true today, there are many people who look to their faith for answers when faced with unimaginable catastrophes.

Chapter 6: The Plague Disappears

While it's true that the bubonic plague is still active today, its power eventually dissipated to the point where it was generally accepted to have "disappeared."

Quarantine

One of the most powerful tools used to combat the spread of the plague was the use of quarantining, which we've already covered in quite some detail. But what might be an important detail to include is that it took quite a long time for quarantine measures to be put in place all around the world.

For example, one of the first documented cases of a ship quarantine happened in 1377 in the city now known as Dubrovnik. The Black Death was already spreading rapidly, and the quarantine there was put in place regardless of whether or not anyone on board was exhibiting symptoms.

However, quarantines didn't become common everywhere until a few hundred years later during subsequent plague outbreaks. In England, quarantines of personal residences weren't implemented until the early 1500s. People were required to hang bales of hay outside their homes to let their community know they were sick. Anyone who had contact with someone infected with the Black Death had to carry a white pole with them whenever they left their house to let others know there was a chance they were carrying the sickness.

Eventually, it became standard practice to shut people into their homes when they were sick. While some places simply expected people to follow the rules, there were other cities that took much more aggressive approaches. When the plague took down a large portion of the population of London during the 1600s, people were either barricaded into their homes or forced into places called pesthouses. It didn't matter if there were healthy people still inside the home; if one person was sick, then everyone would be treated as though they were sick. This was necessary because of the highly contagious nature of the disease. And, of course, at the time, there were no tests available that could detect the presence of the Black Death before symptoms appeared. Their homes would be kept guarded, and anyone who attempted to escape could possibly face death.

Of course, this was not a perfect system. Many people managed to get out of quarantined homes without detection. Plus, although armed guards were used, there weren't enough of them to guard every residence where a sick person lived. So, as a result, sickness was still able to pass through communities quite rapidly.

However, quarantining was definitely a powerful tool in limiting the spread of the plague. In fact, it was so effective that it is still in use today. Just a few years ago, a cruise ship carrying passengers who were sick was kept quarantined for weeks to prevent the spread of disease. Many people have also quarantined when they are sick themselves, which means they are not able to pass illnesses on to as many people as they might if they had gone about their regular lives.

Quarantining isn't just a measure that is useful in the prevention of deadly plagues; it can also be used to help prevent the spread of the common cold. Of course, this type of quarantining doesn't require a hay bale or a cross to be present outside your door, but staying home from work when sick not only can help heal you faster but also help protect your friends and colleagues from catching a cold as well.

Sanitization

The truth is there is no clear answer for why the Black Death eventually died down to a level where it was no longer a major threat. However, there are several theories as to why it began to diminish after hundreds of years of havoc. One of the most likely reasons is the implementation of sanitization systems around the world. Let's take a look at what changes were made and how that impacted not just the spread of the Black Death but also life in general.

As you'll recall, for many years, it was thought that the Black Death had been delivered by God. It was also thought that bad-smelling air was the culprit. Because of this, a lot of the general health and safety measures we now know were not even on anyone's mind in the Middle Ages. It wasn't until the 1700s that disease began to be linked to unsanitary conditions.

Without cities, it might have taken longer for the world to realize that exposure to waste was hazardous to one's health. In small towns, there were fewer people, so even though their attitude toward waste was similar to that of big cities, it didn't pile up in the same way. But by the mid-1800s, the lack of proper sanitization was starting to become a really big issue.

Now, it's important to note that different countries had different approaches to waste. Ancient Rome and Egypt are both examples of places that had developed versions of sewage systems, and some of this knowledge was kept through the years and expanded into other countries. However, even with some systems in place, there was no system that processed or cleansed wastewater. Sewage would generally just be tossed into whatever water source was nearby.

This was a major issue in many countries around the world. Wastewater containing sewage and other toxins would either be dumped into rivers and oceans or sometimes just thrown on the street. Garbage also had no proper method of collection and would typically just be abandoned or sometimes burned.

It wasn't really until the smell of cities and the death toll from a multitude of diseases got really bad that steps were taken to bring in adequate sanitization systems. Of course, there were some people who had championed change for a long time or were instrumental in creating some of these systems. Let's take a look at one of these figures.

Sir John Pringle

Sir John Pringle was an English physician who studied disease. He studied in England and the Netherlands, and his particular area of interest was the spread of disease within hospitals and army camps.

In 1752, he published *Observations on the Diseases of the Army*, which helped lay the groundwork for systems that are still utilized in the military today. A major note of his was the importance of sanitization in military camps, particularly the use of proper restroom facilities and how crucial it was to keep camps as dry as possible. Drainage systems were put in place, and it was highly encouraged that the military stay away from marshes whenever possible.

Sir Pringle also encouraged the use of adequate ventilation systems in hospitals. As you may recall, the demand for proper ventilation has dominated news stories for the past few years. While there have been many suggestions and theories put forward about public health throughout the thousands of years that humans have been on this earth, it's incredible to think that some of the conclusions that were drawn in the past still stand the test of time. Ventilation and staying away from wastewater continue to be two of the best techniques that can help keep a population safe today.

Pringle's work also set the stage for what is known as health surveillance data. This tracks not only diseases related to sanitization and geographic location but also looks at childhood diseases to determine which individuals or groups might be most at risk. This type of data has been instrumental in helping to reduce diseases within the military.

You have to understand that not only was the Black Death still an issue, but there were several other diseases that were commonplace until sanitization took priority. These included typhoid fever, tuberculosis, cholera, and smallpox. In fact, at one point, things got so bad that half of all children within the working class in England died before the age of five. While people in the 1300s perhaps didn't have enough resources to study the spread of disease, a couple of hundred years later, there was a much better understanding of disease. For example, the primary ideas of germ theory had been put forth by Girolamo Fracastoro in 1546, but it wasn't until the 1800s that the idea really took off with a greater understanding of bacteria and how they could cause enormous damage even when they weren't visible to the naked eye. So, an advancement in scientific understanding was a major reason why there were such strides made in sanitization, but there was another reason as well: cities smelled bad. Really bad.

Waste and sewage littered the streets and waterways, and lower-class neighborhoods were overcrowded and filthy. The death and sickness rates were so high that populations were being affected, and many people had to drop out of the workplace. This was particularly evident during the Industrial Revolution when the population in cities grew due to the proliferation of warehouses. With so much production happening, many businesses required large workforces, and thousands of people rushed into big cities in search of jobs. While this improved the lives of many, it also forced large portions of the population into slums and greatly increased the amount of waste.

With the advancements made in science and medicine and an increasingly urgent need for better systems to prevent diseases, a public health proposal came along known as the Sanitary Idea.

For some time, people had been examining the impact of poor sanitation on public health, and it was Villerme, a physician in Paris, who noted that the lower classes seemed to suffer disease at much higher rates than the upper classes. This had been discovered after many unsuccessful attempts to find out why certain areas had such high rates of disease. When things like climate and elevation turned up nothing, he connected economic factors with rates of disease and realized there was an extremely strong correlation.

Around the same time, Sir Edwin Chadwick, who worked as a social reformer, also began looking into these issues. He eventually published a report called "Report into the Sanitary Conditions of the Labouring Populations of Great Britain."

Now, sadly, a lot of these advancements were not necessarily made out of caring for the health of the general population. Instead, Chadwick pointed out that such rampant disease greatly reduced the availability of workers. It was also observed that a sick person cost the government more than a healthy one. So, one could certainly argue that the sanitary measures that were eventually put in place were done in an attempt to protect capitalism and not because the government cared about the health of the working class.

Regardless, these reports did signal a change in public sanitization. Paris and London were the earliest adopters of these improved systems, but cities around the world began to implement better sanitation systems over the next hundred years.

This point in history brought new awareness to the important role that engineers could play in public health. While much of the work surrounding the treatment and prevention of disease was left to scientists, it was engineers who had to design and implement these intricate systems.

A fascinating element to all of this is that the actual science behind a lot of this thinking still wasn't correct. The concept of miasma, which we covered in Chapter 3, was still in vogue during this time. Chadwick himself was a believer in this theory. But of course, many unsanitary conditions did smell, so while the smell wasn't the cause of disease, many of the strategies that got rid of the smell also got rid of a lot of the bacteria that caused these illnesses.

The Sanitary Idea was enormously successful and drastically reduced rates of infection. Along with the introduction of modern sanitary systems, a slew of legislation was passed as well. This legislation put certain rules in place in terms of sewage and waste disposal. It also put requirements on landlords to provide certain standards of living for their tenants.

The success of these ideas has been demonstrated throughout history. People living in clean spaces with good ventilation and proper nutrition are generally healthier. People living in cramped, impoverished areas or living through periods of war often fall victim to disease.

Chadwick's ideas were not immediately accepted. However, the severity of the situation at the time was enough to convince the government to implement them. In his report, for example, it was shown that the average age of death for laborers was sixteen years old. Tradesmen fared just a little better. Their average age of death was twenty-two. Having no other solutions available to them, governments around the world started to improve sanitation and living quarters. The almost immediate success of these changes created a ripple effect, and soon, "being clean" was seen as a sign of virtue and success.

While the shift toward more sanitary living conditions was certainly a smart one, this time period created an unusual issue that still persists in society today. This is the idea that cleanliness indicates moral superiority. In some cases, people believe that cleanliness can even bring one closer to God. However, the idea of cleanliness doesn't always indicate whether or not something is sanitary. People living in poverty may not always have the resources available to properly wash themselves or their clothing. They may also not be able to clean or repair their homes and businesses as well as someone in a higher tax bracket.

However, this difference in appearance does not mean that the individual with less money is unable to maintain proper waste disposal, which is really what the biggest issue is in terms of preventing disease.

Nevertheless, there has been unfair discrimination placed upon people who are unable to keep up with the standards of cleanliness that have become a signal of morality. This is a rather fascinating shift in thinking from hundreds of years earlier when people were more than comfortable spreading feces or putting bare chicken bottoms all over their bodies!

Advancement of Germ Theory

As the 1800s wore on, there were many scientific advancements made that helped shape the course of disease treatment and understanding. One of the most pivotal discoveries made during this time was by Louis Pasteur, a French chemist and biologist. Pasteur was studying food and drink and examined possible reasons for why they spoiled even though nothing visible had happened to them.

After some period of study, he concluded that this must be caused by microorganisms, bacteria that were too small for the human eye to see without the help of a powerful microscope. As you may have already guessed, it was because of him that pasteurization is a common practice today. Pasteurization has saved countless lives and has extended the life of food for people all over the world.

Pasteur helped set the stage for an understanding of where the Black Death came from. Without this knowledge, a treatment could never have been developed, and we might still be dealing with ongoing waves of the disease.

Of course, the waves of the pandemic were much less severe in the 1800s than when they first hit European shores back in 1337, but that doesn't mean the Black Death had disappeared. It was still responsible for claiming countless lives, and any advancements brought the world one step closer to ending it once and for all.

Immunity

There's one final element to the disappearance of the Black Death that's worth mentioning before we close out this chapter. That is the topic of immune systems and their role in diminishing the impact of the plague.

This is an area that has been studied, but given that the worst waves of the Black Death happened so long ago and there have been so many changes since then, it is hard to draw any definite conclusions. However, the topic of immunity is still worth mentioning when talking about the Black Death and disease in general.

With the exception of a few different disorders, the human body is typically made up of twenty-three pairs of chromosomes (making forty-six in total). Within these chromosomes lies our genes, which are made up of DNA. Our genes are basically little instruction manuals for our bodies. They determine our features, such as the color of our eyes and the size of our nose. But they also determine how our body responds to disease and environmental factors.

The Black Death is incredibly aggressive. Before treatments became available, there was a very high chance that anyone who contracted it would be dead within three days. But there were some who survived it. And there were others who never got it at all, even though they were exposed to it multiple times. Why is that?

One thought is that people who avoided or survived the Black Death might have had specific gene variants that protected against the disease. A variant may also be referred to as a mutation that can occur in a gene. These mutations can then be passed down through the family line, which means that future generations may be born with natural immunity against something like the Black Death.

This is a phenomenon that is known as natural selection. It has been extensively studied in animal populations. While many people like to prescribe the idea of "survival of the fittest" to situations like this, it actually has nothing to do with fitness. This has been demonstrated many times when the world has faced other pandemics. People who had no prior history of disease, exercised frequently, and had a healthy diet were often just as susceptible to the disease as people who did not follow such strict diet and fitness regimens. Of course, the situation is very different for people who already have a disability or compromised immune system.

Natural selection is something that happens because people happen to be born with certain genes. Also, just because one person might have a gene variant that naturally protects them against the bubonic plague does not mean that that same variant can protect them from any other diseases. It just depends on whether certain mutations are helpful at protecting against the specific bacterium present in whichever disease is prevalent at the time.

Recently, two scientists, Dr. Hendrik Poinar from McMaster University in Canada and Dr. Luis Barreiro from the University of Chicago in the United States, set out to research this exact topic. They managed to access the remains of five hundred people who lived before, during, and after the first wave of the Black Death in Europe back in the 1300s. They procured most of the samples from cemeteries in England and a few from locations in Denmark. Their final conclusions were drawn from the samples of two hundred people.

The way this research was conducted was by looking at specific variants that appeared to have either increased or decreased dramatically after the Black Death swept through the area. Dr. Poinar and Dr. Barreiro ended up observing four variants of interest. After further investigation, they found that there was one particular variant located near the gene ERAP2, which is responsible for the production of a protein that helps a pathogen protein break into smaller pieces. This then supports the immune system in being more efficient at noticing infections. People who had two of this specific variant had an even better chance of fighting off infection. This was because the macrophages (a type of white blood cell that can kill microorganisms and help support healthy immune systems) were better at attacking the bacterium that caused the Black Death (*Y. pestis*) with the support of the variant.

Although the variant in question seemed to help protect against the Black Death, it had its downside as well, as it created an elevated risk of Crohn's disease. There was also another variant that seemed to offer enhanced protection against the Black Death, but that variant also came with a great risk of two types of autoimmune diseases. So, while the populations affected by the Black Death might have developed better resistance to it over the generations, natural selection might mean that much of the world also became more likely to end up with certain autoimmune diseases.

Many questions remain about why and how the Black Death disappeared, but that is often the case with horrific and mystifying pandemics that come in and out of our lives. What we do know is that the plague reshaped the course of history and resulted in some long-lasting social changes for the better.

Chapter 7: Shaping the Course of European History

There's no way to know what the world would have looked like had the Black Death never happened. Instead, all we can do is observe all the changes that happened as a result of it.

One of the biggest changes that resulted from the bubonic plague was a change in class systems. While we've already talked in some detail about the plague-affected labor, there are a few terms that we haven't yet covered. Labor is one of the most studied areas of this time period, and what happened as a result of labor shortages set the stage for labor disputes that still happen in a similar way today. Let's get into a few terms you should know about.

Feudal System

The feudal system, or feudalism, was in place in Europe for centuries. It began sometime in the 700s and remained a powerful system up into the 1400s. Although this system began to diminish around that time, it continued to remain in place in some areas for another four hundred years!

This system was put in place to provide the upper class with a way to exert and retain their power. Under the feudal system, parcels of land, known as fiefs, would be loaned out to a tenant. However, instead of just paying rent (which was definitely a requirement as well), it was expected that whoever was occupying the land would do the landowner's bidding. This could mean a wide range of services. A large reason for developing the feudal system was to ensure a strong enough army would be at the ready. Someone occupying a fief was required to join in any military operations that were required of them.

This system created a huge imbalance in society. Instead of laws being put in place by an elected government, almost all the power was put in the hands of the individual lords in charge of the fiefs. They held the ultimate power over the people below them.

Now, you may be wondering why some people within the feudal system simply couldn't come and go as they pleased. Unfortunately, it wasn't quite as simple as that. There definitely were some people who were in a comfortable enough position to decide whether or not they wanted to pay a higher rent or exchange services for the land they lived on. This exchange sometimes even happens today. Someone might be a building manager in exchange for free rent or offer to do repairs or some gardening in exchange for a rent reduction. However, at the bottom of the change were serfs.

Serfdom was the lowest level of the feudal system. This was when people were born onto these specific plots of land or were paid such extraordinarily low wages that they had no hope of ever advancing in the world. Because of this, they were forever tied to the lords who owned the land and were forced into doing whatever work was demanded of them, even if it was completely unreasonable.

This was the system that was in place when the Black Death first sailed into port. Serfs were not technically bound to a person, but they were bound to the land. They cultivated their own food and necessities but were obligated to give most of their harvest to their lord. The lords also determined how they managed the land and where they milled their wheat.

Not only was the work a serf did determined by their lord, but so was everything else. Serfs were not allowed to leave their area of residence or change their occupation unless they received permission from their lord. Not only that, but they couldn't even marry someone of their own choosing unless their lord approved of it. Generally, a serf's only hope at freedom was through escape. Lords were notoriously brutal and not generally known to be compassionate.

Once the worker population shrank, the feudal system began to crash, and the lower classes finally began to make the earnings they deserved. Of course, we have covered the rest of that in an earlier chapter, but now you know more about the exact conditions landowners were attempting to force people back into.

The end of the feudal system was one of the biggest changes that resulted from the Black Death. The exploitation of workers is sadly one that continues to this day, but the peasant revolt helped to undo some of the power landowners once had. Today, most of the places where feudalism was once the norm now have strict rules against serfdom and give much more power to workers. France, in particular, is known to have quite a robust working culture. This might not have been the case today if the Black Death had never happened.

Women

Even though the Black Death started hundreds of years ago, it still generates an incredible amount of interest among historians. However, documentation from the time has sometimes been difficult to acquire, and there have been many disagreements on a variety of topics. One such topic is how the Black Death affected the lives of women.

For a long time, the idea was put forth that the years following the first wave of the Black Death were known as the "golden years" for women. This was because so many women, who had very few rights before the pandemic, were suddenly in a position to support themselves and build up their assets. With so many workers dead, landowners would inevitably be willing to turn to anyone to get work done, even if that meant employing women.

However, while it is certainly true that there must have been more job openings available after the first wave, it doesn't follow that landowners would go to women. And if they did, it seems likely that women were handed the short end of the stick.

At the time, it was common for a lot of work to be delivered under short-term contracts. This might mean a weekly contract or even something as short as a day. These contracts were generally more lucrative than the annual contracts that tied a worker to one position and often involved housing. While many men pursued short-term work for higher pay, it seemed that women tended to end up in fixed contracts that gave them less money and less freedom.

The exact reasons for this difference between male and female workers are unclear, but it could be due to the established societal preference for male workers and the uncertainty of whether or not short-term work would be consistently available. Annual work might have paid less, but at least it could provide security to a woman whose position was already precarious.

Of course, it is likely that some women ended up in a better position than others after the arrival of the Black Death, but there doesn't seem to be much evidence to suggest that this happened in large enough numbers to have made a great difference for women in the long term. This is supported by the fact that the rights of women remained fairly unchanged for many years, even after the impact of the Black Death began to lessen. But we still don't know everything about what happened during that time. So, it's nice to imagine that some women saw a benefit after so much darkness.

However, there is one area of a woman's life that did see a positive change due to the pandemic, and that was the issue of inheritance.

Before the Black Death, it was very unusual for women to be able to own land. Most inheritance laws dictated that land and other assets could only be left to a son. If no son had been produced, then the inheritance would be passed on to the next closest male relative.

However, because so many people died during the Black Death, it became impossible to operate under the same inheritance system. Because of this, many women ended up owning land for the first time. Not only that, but some of them were able to own and run their own businesses and even have some decision-making power over who they decided to marry.

However, these new freedoms did not last forever. After the initial panic of the plague had passed, many governments and religious institutions began to claw back the rights they had temporarily granted to women. The idea that men were the only ones capable of running homes or government was still prevalent, and it would be hundreds of years before most women would be able to own property again. For instance, it wasn't until 1900 that laws were passed in every US state that allowed women the right to their own money or the ability to have property in their own name. However, any movement, even if not immediately successful, lays the groundwork for future ones. The freedom that women enjoyed, even if temporary, surely influenced women's rights in the future.

Art

As previously mentioned, artistic expression was incredibly important during the Black Death. During this time, there was a noted increase in motifs of death. A lot of the artwork made during the plague was very dark and, interestingly, much less grand than a lot of the work that had been produced prior to the pandemic.

Architecture

Another area that experienced a drastic change was the design of architecture. As the world gradually began to better understand how the disease moved through the world, there was a need to redesign cities and buildings.

Many cities expanded. A lot of them had grown overcrowded, with many people in the lower classes forced into extremely cramped and unsanitary housing. When the world started to understand that ventilation and good sanitation were important tools to help combat the plague, more housing began to be built to spread out the population. There was also an emphasis on providing larger outdoor spaces within cities, where people could breathe in fresh air without being crammed together inside.

The Black Death also required the construction of several plague hospitals. These were meant to be sanitary, organized buildings where people could be isolated from the healthy and die a dignified death. While not every hospital lived up to these ideals, the outline of these hospitals helped to serve as a blueprint for future medical facilities.

But it wasn't just the design of a city that changed during and after the pandemic. It was the actual buildings themselves.

Before the Black Death began to ravage Europe, architecture had been quite elaborate. French Gothic was the dominant style. It is known for its large pointed arches and windows. Notre-Dame Cathedral is a well-known example of a beautiful French Gothic building. However, after the Black Death, there was a marked decline in this opulent style. Instead, construction trended toward what is now known as Perpendicular Gothic. This style was very different from the style that had been so beloved before. It was quite simple and featured much harsher angles and lines. There were very few decorative embellishments, and buildings took on a rather cold and authoritarian-looking appearance.

Architecture has changed throughout time, and it's not uncommon for trends to shift after a major event, but what's interesting is trying to determine why specific styles came into vogue. There are a few theories.

Some historians suggest that the change in architecture had little to do with the plague at all. It's suggested that perpendicular designs were already becoming fashionable even before the Black Death arrived and that this change was falsely attributed to being a result of the plague instead of a natural change in trends.

Another theory is that this change in architecture was connected to the massive loss of life experienced during the pandemic. It is thought that the shift was due to the loss of experts in the architectural field. French Gothic designs are so elaborate and detailed that it took workers many years to perfect their craft. It is possible that many people with the know-how in these areas died and that to continually build in this style after the Black Death simply wasn't possible.

A third suggested theory regards cost. The plague saw a drastic increase in inflation, as well as a desperate demand for critical workers in areas like agriculture. This might have meant that the construction of beautiful and elaborate buildings was no longer economically feasible. The sharp and angular buildings of the Perpendicular Gothic period could have been the result of cost-cutting labor.

Whatever the reason, Perpendicular Gothic, also eventually known as Tudor architecture, remained the dominant style until the shift to Renaissance architecture in the mid-1500s.

Shift in Beliefs

As was mentioned in Chapter 5, religion played a major role in the response to the Black Death. However, it is unlikely that religious leaders foresaw the dip in faith that resulted from the dreadful disease.

The powerlessness of the church to prevent the Black Death from spreading created a lot of anger and resentment toward God and religious leaders. This divide took quite some time for the church to repair. Its efforts were also hampered because so many priests had died. While it would be inaccurate to say that the church lost its power, it definitely saw a decline in numbers, as many people turned toward other forms of spirituality or to more extremist groups, such as the flagellant movement.

What might be a more accurate statement is that many people lost their belief in the church. The core beliefs of Catholicism remained instilled in the general population of Europe, but a lot of the dissatisfaction was directed at the church. People were looking for solace and the ability to be absolved of their sins, but the steep decline of available clergymen made doing this difficult. While this wasn't within the church's control, it didn't stop Catholics from being angry about it and seeking comfort in whatever ways they could.

To further illustrate the difficulties the Catholic Church found itself in, it's important to talk about how many clergymen died. Across certain parts of England, the number of dead hovered at around 50 percent, while in one diocese in Barcelona, clergymen faced a 60 percent death rate at the peak of the plague. It has even been suggested that leaders of the church were infected and died at higher numbers than the general public due to the fact that they were constantly comforting and praying for the sick.

While the church gradually began to return to its former glory, the shifting ideas about how it should operate had already gone into motion. New congregations were formed, and many Catholics began to redefine their expectations of the church and religion. While not the sole cause, this shift in attitude helped lead to the Reformation in the 1500s. This was a religious revolution that led to the formation of Protestantism, another major branch of Christianity. One of the core beliefs during the beginning of Protestantism was that the Catholic Church was corrupt and had drifted away from the most important values of the faith. Thus, Protestantism was created with the idea of righting the wrongs that had been done and creating a purer faith.

This, of course, led to other independent faith movements. Again, these movements were not in opposition to the idea of God himself but rather the dominant power that had been placed in the hands of the Catholic Church for so long.

The Black Death created enormous shifts in the political, social, and economic landscape of Europe. While many norms shifted during this time, the ones covered in this chapter were some of the most striking and well documented.

Chapter 8: Scientific Advancements in the Wake of the Black Death

The Black Death continues to fascinate scientists and the general public to this very day. For a long time, the cause of it was completely misunderstood. It was seen as a punishment from God or as an evil that had simply floated in on a wave of bad air.

You might also recall the theory of the four humors, which persisted for generations.

However, as time wore on and the bubonic plague continued to come back every few years, there were some who grew understandably skeptical. If the plague really was a punishment from God or was simply the imbalance of fluids within the body, then why didn't it go away after repenting one's sins or draining one's blood?

It took a long time for germ theory to gain significant traction. Throughout the 1600s and 1700s, there had been discussions on the topic. In 1665, Robert Hooke was able to accurately tell the world about how the fruiting structures of molds worked. And just over a decade later, Antoni van Leeuwenhoek discovered bacteria. However, despite these promising discoveries, it would still take over two hundred years for the official cause of the Black Death to be found.

The 19th century is when several major advancements in the understanding of infectious diseases were made. Up until this point, the prevailing theory around disease was that it was the result of something called spontaneous generation.

Spontaneous generation is the idea that life (and bacteria is included within that) could just appear spontaneously. For example, someone who believed in this theory might think that mice would just appear in food that had been left out or that maggots would simply arise out of the flesh of a decaying corpse. This idea that life could arrive spontaneously, sometimes out of non-living matter, was essential in discovering the real cause of how the Black Death worked.

Louis Pasteur wasn't convinced that spontaneous generation was true, so he set out to conduct some experiments to contradict the theory. In one experiment, he prepared some broth within a special compartment that was completely sealed off from any outside air. Pasteur had already been exploring germ theory and fermentation for some time, so he was already a full believer in germ theory. But if the idea of spontaneous generation was true, then the broth should have been able to spoil even within its air-sealed compartment.

However, Pasteur's guess about spontaneous generation turned out to be correct. When the broth remained sealed, it showed no sign of being impacted by microorganisms. It didn't spoil, instead remaining uncontaminated. But when Pasteur finally broke the seal, the liquid almost instantly started to spoil.

This experiment opened the door to a much greater understanding of how disease happens. Pasteur's work created massive changes in safety standards around food. Once it was known that disease and fermentation happened because of an outside source, it was much easier to work on methods to prevent this. His work eventually led to his discovery of pasteurization. This is a process that has made many products, including wine, eggs, and milk, much safer to consume. Before pasteurization, it was not uncommon to contract serious illnesses due to bacteria in different food products. Raw milk was a particularly vicious culprit.

Today, many countries have laws around pasteurization and the sale of raw milk. While the sale of raw milk in the United States is allowed under certain circumstances, it is under fairly strict regulation, and for good reason. Raw milk can carry salmonella, staph, and listeria, among many other harmful bacteria. A study of illnesses connected to the consumption of raw milk in the United States between the years 1998 and 2018 saw that raw milk was responsible for 202 different outbreaks. These outbreaks caused 2,645 illnesses and over 200 hospitalizations. It was also found that areas that allowed the sale of raw milk saw over three times the number of outbreaks than areas where the sale of raw milk was prohibited. This study demonstrated the effectiveness of both pasteurization and laws regulating the sale of raw milk.

Pasteurization has evolved since first being developed, and there are two different ways that it is commonly done. In the United States, most milk is pasteurized in a process known as high-temperature short-time pasteurization (HTST). HTST is able to be performed on large quantities of milk at the same time, which is cost-effective and, therefore, an attractive process for dairy producers. However, this type of pasteurization, while still getting rid of bacteria, doesn't have a very long shelf life. It generally needs to be consumed within a few weeks, and it has to be refrigerated to remain safe to drink.

Outside of North America, the most popular form of pasteurization is something called ultra-heat-treated pasteurization, or UHT for short. This pasteurization process heats milk to a higher temperature than is used in HTST, which also results in a slightly different taste than the milk you might be used to drinking in the United States. UHT milk does not need to be refrigerated and can last for three months on the shelf.

This advancement in the understanding of germ theory led to other food safety measures, including the treatment of eggs. Once again, the choice of treatment varies greatly between the North American approach and the approach many European countries and other areas of the world take when it comes to preventing serious foodborne illnesses.

One of the main concerns related to the consumption of eggs is the risk of salmonella. Salmonella contamination is most commonly caused by bacteria that make their way onto an eggshell. This is due to the excess of ground material and feces that are often found in chicken coops and factories. Salmonella might also appear underneath the shell if the laying hen is experiencing an internal infection.

Because of the risk of salmonella, it became common practice in North America for egg producers to put all of their eggs through a vigorous cleaning process as soon as they were laid. This rids the shells of any harmful bacteria and, in theory, makes them safe for consumption.

However, this process does end up causing another potential problem, as it rids the egg of a small protective layer known as a cuticle. A cuticle is what helps the egg protect itself from bacteria passing through the shell and into the egg, which opens up the possibility of salmonella still being present inside the egg. Because of this, eggs in North America need to be refrigerated, and it is recommended that all eggs be cooked before consumption.

In Europe, there is a law prohibiting the washing of eggs in order to keep that cuticle intact. Eggs are kept on the shelf instead of the fridge. This is to prevent bacteria from forming inside the egg when switching between cold and warm temperatures.

Both methods have seen reductions in foodborne illnesses. However, it's hard to determine if one method is superior. The differences in population numbers make it hard to get comparable studies. Nevertheless, these kinds of changes within food safety can be traced back to the theory that helped discover the bacterium behind the Black Death.

Of course, with any advancement in science, there comes a group of skeptics. When the pasteurization of milk was first suggested in the state of New York, it was met with a fair amount of resistance. It was not until rates of foodborne illnesses dramatically decreased that it began to become widely adopted all over the country.

Even today, there are some groups who claim that pasteurized milk is harmful or less nutritional than raw milk. These claims have generally been made by individuals with no scientific background, and they have all been dismissed by the major health organizations in the United States.

Another area that underwent a major transformation in part because of the Black Death was the healthcare system as a whole. Prior to the Black Death making its way through Europe, a lot of medical professionals operated at an individual level. There was very little oversight, and the idea of regulations put in place for the health of all of society wasn't particularly common.

After the recommendations regarding sanitation measures were made by Edwin Chadwick, cities around the world started reevaluating the way they looked at public health. While the understanding at the time was still focused on the theory of miasma, changes made at this time set the stage for health agencies today.

Health surveys became commonplace. These looked at different areas and measured the rates of diseases within them to help determine what was causing an increase in illness or death within different populations. This is a practice that continues today and is incredibly useful for helping to initiate social change. Health surveys are done through things like the census or by measuring wastewater in different areas to detect rates of disease.

This type of work eventually led to the creation of various health agencies, as well as better oversight and sanitation procedures in hospitals. This, in turn, also helped develop better water management systems, which helped reduce the number of people falling ill from contaminated drinking water.

All of this work spiraled off into other positive advancements in healthcare systems. In the United States, there was an increased interest in funding institutions that were specifically designed to assist individuals who were struggling with their mental health. Before, it had been common to simply shut people with mental health issues in jail, but throughout the late 1800s, many mental health facilities were opened with the express purpose of helping to cope with this issue.

Unfortunately, these early institutions were not particularly helpful. They frequently practiced extremely troubling and ineffective methods, such as electroshock therapy and lobotomies. However, this early separation of mental health institutions from the criminal justice system laid the groundwork for the many transformative and helpful mental health facilities around the world today.

Vinegar and Heat

As you might remember from our chapter on the various cures and treatments people used during the early waves of the Black Death, there were many questionable ingredients. A lot of this was due to the misunderstanding about how exactly the disease was contracted. However, even though the theories behind a few of the methods were incorrect, it turns out that not all of the treatments people tried were useless.

One of the most popular tonics that was applied during the Black Death was the four thieves' vinegar tonic. It was rumored that rubbing it on one's body would prevent the plague from infecting you. This is not entirely true, but there is some validity to vinegar's disinfecting powers.

A study from 2014 found that acetic acid, which is the active ingredient within vinegar, can be an effective killer of mycobacteria. This study was specifically conducted on the bacterium that causes tuberculosis after it had been exposed to acetic acid for thirty minutes.

Although this was an exciting discovery, there are some drawbacks. Vinegar may be effective against certain bacteria, but it is not as powerful and reliable as commercial-grade disinfectants. It also is generally not capable of killing as high a percentage of bacteria as something like bleach. However, its beneficial disinfecting qualities can be of great use to those who may not be in a position to afford commercial products. Vinegar is also less hazardous than other disinfectants, which can sometimes create highly toxic fumes if used incorrectly. (This can also happen with vinegar as well. The combination of vinegar and bleach can quickly create a highly poisonous chlorine gas that can be lethal.)

While vinegar may not be the right choice as a disinfectant everywhere, it certainly has its benefits. During the Black Death, it was often used as a preventative rub as opposed to a cleanser, which might have made it more effective for people hoping to escape the plague. It is very likely that vinegar played a part in helping some people avoid infection, and it's a cheap and effective tool for helping people stay safer from disease today.

Another method that wasn't used correctly but still had some validity to it was the use of fire to dispel or prevent disease. While it was thought that fire would rid a person of disease, the actual benefit behind using heat to combat the plague is that high heat is capable of killing bacteria. That's why it's recommended that you cook something like chicken, which is a common culprit in foodborne illnesses.

Although Pope Clement VI likely avoided the Black Death due to his continual isolation, the constant state of heat in his chambers might have helped protect him from bacteria if anyone else entered the room.

Heat is one of the most effective methods we have against disease today. As you have already learned, pasteurization is a method that uses high heat to prevent bacterial growth. Heat is also a commonly used method for the sterilization of medical equipment. While other methods, such as disinfectants, are used as well, a lot of tools are cleaned using a hot steaming method.

Citizens also use heat to protect themselves every day. People boil water, cook food, and sterilize health products in boiling water to protect themselves from contracting infections. It's a simple, effective, and affordable tool to keep everyone safe.

Although heat is a legitimate method of destroying bacteria, it's important to know the specific requirements of your situation. Depending on what you're trying to clean and what your elevation is, different items need different amounts of time to be considered safe. It is also necessary that food or non-edible items be sanitized in temperatures that are over 149 degrees Fahrenheit. You might be interested to know that this is actually below boiling temperature. However, boiling is often a good measurement to know that you have reached the correct temperature without having to reach for a thermometer.

Epidemiology

In loose terms, epidemiology is the study of the patterns and spread of disease. Throughout history, physicians have sought to find some logic and understanding behind why diseases spread so fast or why some people seem to get sick while others manage to escape an illness.

For a long time, a lot of early epidemiology was tied to guesswork, religion, and observations one could make with the naked eye. It wasn't until the late 1600s that a microscope was created that was powerful enough to see some of the bacteria we now know are responsible for disease.

A major shift in the field of epidemiology came along with Dr. John Snow's discoveries. Because of his findings, it was determined that cholera was spread through contaminated water. Some water in London began to be treated with chlorine, and the rates of cholera decreased.

A few decades after Snow's conclusions surrounding cholera, Joseph Lister began disinfecting medical instruments and a patient's wounds before surgery, which greatly reduced septic shock during medical procedures. This is now standard practice all over the world.

Also in the 1800s were the experiments of Robert Koch. He further supported germ theory by making the discovery that specific germs were responsible for diseases like cholera, anthrax, and tuberculosis.

We have already covered Pasteur's contributions to food safety due to his study of fermentation and work that demonstrated the spontaneous generation theory was incorrect. But there was another major contribution Pasteur made to science and the understanding and prevention of disease: the creation of vaccines.

In the late 1800s, Pasteur was gifted a laboratory by the French government. The lab was given to him in the hopes that he could direct his energy into studying diseases.

At this time, the first vaccination had already taken place, but it hadn't followed the same science that became standard up until a few years ago when RNA vaccines stepped into the spotlight.

For some time, it had been thought that the best way to prevent disease was to purposefully expose yourself to it. Things like "measles parties" have gone in and out of fashion, although they are incorrect ways to protect yourself against disease. While it's true that surviving a disease might potentially provide your body with immunity against it, that still requires you to withstand the initial infection, something that not everyone manages to achieve. Plus, the long-term effects of any kind of infection might be extremely detrimental to one's health.

So, during the 1800s, when it was still thought that exposure might be the best cure, a farmer named Benjamin Jesty began to experiment with cowpox to prevent the contraction of smallpox. At the time, smallpox was a very serious killer, typically leaving 30 percent of those infected dead.

Jesty had previously heard stories about how those who had been infected with cowpox, a skin infection that is common in farm animals, were incapable of contracting smallpox.

Incredibly, without any kind of scientific background, Jesty took it upon himself to purposefully infect his wife and children with a cowpox lesion he had discovered on one of his barnyard animals. Remarkably, this technique proved to be effective and is now generally accepted as the starting point of modern-day vaccines.

It's worth noting that this discovery is often attributed to a physician named Edward Jenner. Jenner did indeed do further testing to confirm that cowpox was effective in combating smallpox infection, but this was done several years later on the basis of Jesty's work.

Years later, when Pasteur started working in the lab, he went back to this first vaccine and decided to dedicate his research to finding vaccines for other diseases. He reasoned that if one had been found for smallpox, then it made sense that all diseases must have something that was a successful combatant against it.

While he initially chose to study a few different forms of disease, he eventually narrowed in on a specific type of cholera that affects chickens. In the beginning, he experimented by purposefully infecting the chickens with live versions of the cholera culture, but after multiple trials, he ended with the same results each time: the chickens would get sick, and many of them would die.

Despite Pasteur's impressive scientific history and incredible genius, one of the best elements of the story of how he found the vaccine is the fact that it happened partly by chance.

After some time experimenting, Pasteur happened to leave town for a few days. When he got back to town, he injected the chickens with the culture as he had many times before, except none of them became sick this time.

While he had been away, the cultures themselves had died, therefore rendering them unable to infect their host. Now, this is where a moment in history was truly created. Pasteur could have, very understandably, assumed that the cultures were useless. Once he realized they were dead, it would have made perfect sense for him to start over with a live culture and continue to go down the wrong path of exploration. However, even though it was clear that he was working with an attenuated culture, he decided to continue experimenting. And he decided to inject the healthy chickens with a live culture of fowl cholera.

What happened next changed everything: the chickens didn't get sick. Pasteur then realized that a harmless version of a bacteria or virus had the potential to protect the immune system from developing infection. In May 1881, he put this to the test in front of a public audience.

Pasteur took an attenuated (weakened or dead) version of anthrax and injected it into sheep, some cows, and a goat. He also had the same amount and distribution of animals who were not injected with the weakened anthrax and used them as the control group in the experiment.

A few weeks later, Pasteur and the audience once again met for the second part of the experiment. This was when Pasteur injected all of the animals with the live bacterium. Just two days later, the ramifications of Pasteur's discovery were clear. All of the control animals were either sick or dead, and all the animals who had been inoculated two weeks earlier were in perfectly good health.

This early success in Pasteur's vaccine experiments led him to work on diseases that also affected humans. He soon created an effective rabies vaccine, and from that point on, public support for vaccine research grew tremendously. Vaccines eventually went on to be developed for a variety of diseases, such as polio, hepatitis A and B, and mumps. The discovery of vaccines changed the course of medical history and has saved countless lives. The yearly flu vaccine that people get all over the world is a result of the development of a vaccine due to the widespread death toll of the 1918 Spanish flu. It is an incredibly important tool for the prevention of disease, and many people consider Pasteur to be a hero.

Discovery of Y. pestis and a Cure for the Black Death

Now, after everything you've learned about the death tolls and the troubling outcomes of the bubonic plague, let's dive into how its cause was discovered and how an effective treatment was eventually developed.

As you may remember from our opening chapter, the origin of the plague was discovered by Alexandre Yersin in 1894. Yersin himself spent some time at the Institut Pasteur, where he spent some time working on vaccine innovation. He and Émile Roux share in the discovery of the diphtheria toxin. However, it is Yersin's discovery of the bacterium responsible for the Black Death for which he is the most famous.

Incredibly, within just two years of Yersin's discovery, an effective antiserum was already being used to treat patients who had become ill with the Black Death. This thorough understanding of the cause of the disease was the true beginning of the end for its hold on the world.

Antiserum, which is a treatment made up of blood that contains the antibodies necessary to fight against the disease, was the standard method for combating the Black Death up until the 1930s when antiserum treatments were replaced by a drug that inhibited the multiplication of *Y. pestis*. Over the next twenty years, further treatments were developed that eventually led to the standard and effective antibiotic treatment that is still used to this day.

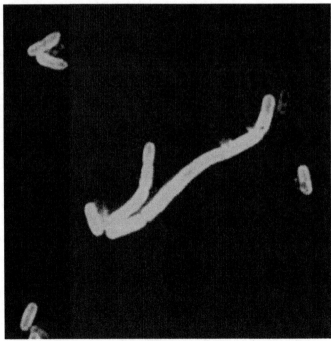

An image of Y. Pestis.
https://commons.wikimedia.org/wiki/File:Yersinia_pestis_fluorescent.jpeg

After Yersin's discovery, a vaccine was also developed to aid in the prevention of the Black Death. Although the vaccines were also effective, they weren't as widely used as some other vaccines. By this point in time, the rates of the plague were already diminishing, and the use of the vaccines was predominantly reserved for soldiers who were serving in areas where there were higher rates of the disease. Today, there is almost no continued use of the Black Death vaccine. Instead, people simply have to take a course of antibiotics to rid themselves of symptoms.

While the plague is treatable today, it can still lead to death if not attended to fast enough. Outcomes are best if antibiotics are prescribed within twenty-four hours of symptoms appearing, so it's very important that anyone who suspects they have contracted the disease gets to a doctor or emergency room immediately.

Today, the United States usually sees around seven cases of the bubonic plague each year. It is typically found in more rural areas, where it may have been passed onto humans by animals. Serious outbreaks of the disease are unlikely thanks to effective treatments, but it's still important that it be taken seriously. If someone can't access or afford treatment, then it could be possible for the disease to spread quickly, so fast treatment must be available for everyone so we can keep the horrors of the Black Death in the past.

While the Black Death was the most destructive pandemic in history, it helped create medical innovations and sanitation systems that have changed the world for the better. Without such a tragic loss of life, there might not have existed the same interest in epidemiology or an insistence on social change. While it was a horrible event that continued for hundreds of years, it arguably changed the world for the better.

Chapter 9: Economic and Social Consequences

The Black Death had enormous economic and social consequences on the lives of people around the world. In Europe, Asia, and North Africa, there was almost no one who had not been impacted by the Black Death. Many of the conversations surrounding the impacts of the Black Death are focused on the economy, such as the changes that happened in the labor market. These are important conversations to have, and we will review the importance of this matter later on in this chapter. However, there is another matter that doesn't always get the attention it deserves: the impact the Black Death had on people's mental health.

It's only very recently that the stigma around mental health has begun to fade away. For a long time, conditions like depression and anxiety, as well as psychiatric disorders, were seen as something embarrassing and shameful. Many people hid their diagnoses or tried to pretend they didn't have them. Thankfully, society is finally starting to talk about mental health issues in earnest. While we still have a long way to go, there is a lot more understanding about mental health than there has ever been.

However, if we are only just now fully beginning to accept the importance of taking care of one's mental health in the year 2023, you can probably imagine what kind of resources might have been available to someone living through an unprecedented pandemic in the year 1337.

To better understand the impact the Black Death had on mental health, let's first look at what trauma does to the brain.

Trauma is defined as a deeply distressing or disturbing experience. Trauma can be a singular event or an ongoing one. While some people might believe that trauma is something that is simply experienced and then let go of, it has been shown that trauma can actually change the chemistry of your brain.

When someone is in a safe environment, they are able to effectively use their prefrontal cortex. This is the planning part of the brain. It helps with rational thought and decision-making. Its smooth operation is crucial to help keep us safe and make logical decisions.

When we experience a traumatic event, the prefrontal cortex is not able to function the way it should. Instead, it goes into a circuit of fear. When the prefrontal cortex is in this mode, it is very difficult for a person to think or act rationally. They might get angry, go numb and shut down, physically run away, or mentally disassociate.

This natural response to trauma can be very difficult for people who have never experienced this phenomenon to understand. It has caused many problems during court cases when victims of physical or sexual attacks take the stand. Often, due to this disruption to a victim's prefrontal cortex, they might not act in the way you think they "should." However, their ability for rational thought was severely compromised due to the trauma they experienced.

Trauma can also have a profound effect on memory. During this state, your brain is not able to process and encode memories the way it normally does, so it is very common for people who've experienced trauma to have a lot of gaps in their recollection of events. Sometimes, entire events will be blank in someone's mind.

Of course, the hope is that someone who has experienced severe trauma is able to access the help they need. However, those kinds of medical professionals were not widely available during the Middle Ages. While therapeutic practices have been documented since ancient Greece, it simply wasn't common practice to receive help for trauma during the Black Death. Plus, with such a drastic loss of life, getting help for even the most basic needs was often a challenge since so many physicians died.

In a paper by Erin Carty, it's discussed how the plague completely altered people's demeanor. The Black Death was such an indiscriminate killer. It didn't matter what your age, race, religion, or economic status was; it came for everyone. This created an enormous sense of panic, paranoia, and hopelessness.

This feeling is evident in the response that many Catholics had toward their church during the pandemic. The church saw a devastating loss of clergymen, which resulted in the institution not being able to see to the needs of all of its members. Some parishes completely shut down, and others were overwhelmed with requests for Mass, funeral ceremonies, and absolution.

Whatever your relationship is with the church, you may expect that Catholics would have had some sympathy for the unprecedented situation in which the church found itself. The loss of life within the church had not been through any fault of its own. In fact, as mentioned earlier, the large number of dead within the church might have been due to the clergy's overexposure to the sick as they attempted to bring their followers some comfort in their final days.

However, compassion was not the response given by many members of the church. Instead, the church was blamed for its lack of numbers and its inability to meet the demands made upon it. Members sought other means of comfort, such as joining the controversial flagellant movement or starting new branches of Christianity. While there were certainly some who must have already been dissatisfied with the church prior to the start of the Black Death, it is interesting to wonder how many would have had such a visceral response to the church's troubles had the entire continent not experienced severe trauma at the same time.

One of the effects that trauma had on the people who lived through the Black Death was an increased preference for isolation. The fear of contracting the disease was so great that being on one's own became the only way some people knew how to survive. This was, of course, exacerbated by the extensive quarantines that people were required to abide by. While quarantines are a necessary preventative measure to limit the spread of disease, they can also have profound impacts on people's mental health. Human beings thrive on connection. Human touch is essential for one's health and happiness. In fact, touch is so important that babies who don't receive enough physical contact from their parents can get sick, have stunted development, or even die.

Some of the people who lived through the pandemic might have also been quarantined with loved ones who died. In some cases, people might have ended up barricaded in their homes with deceased loved ones for weeks. This unimaginable horror adds an almost unbearable weight to an already difficult situation.

People who suffer from trauma can go on to develop a host of mental health issues, such as a dependency on alcohol and sex addiction. Without any resources for treatment back in the day, many people suffered from these issues for the rest of their lives.

Another social consequence that developed out of the trauma of the Black Death was an increase in xenophobia and antisemitism. While we have already touched on the antisemitism that ran rampant during the Black Death, there was also a general distrust and suspicion of immigrants and even people who came from different regions or towns.

When people are scared or angry, they often look for someone to blame. When there is no one person or group who can be held responsible, people often decide to blame whoever seems or looks different than them. So, people began to blame people from other places or people who were in a lower class than they were. This is a pattern that has been repeated throughout history. We've witnessed it very recently with the drastic increase in hate crimes perpetrated against those of Asian descent.

Sadly, this behavior only further contributes to feelings of paranoia and loneliness, but again, many people weren't able to think straight. In difficult times, people search for a sense of control. For some, that might mean helping others, but for many, it means placing blame and pushing people away. It sometimes even results in violence.

People became increasingly protective of their own communities. In some areas of Europe, visitors were required to go through an intensive inspection process, and in some cases, they were not even allowed within city limits. This was especially true of tradesmen, who, while providing an essential service, were often blamed for the spread of the plague.

Nobody experiences trauma in the same way. For some, living through the Black Death made them a better, more compassionate person. It brought them closer to their faith and gave them a renewed appreciation for life. But for many others, it shattered their sense of self and their relationship to the world around them. Many experienced complete breakdowns and completely withdrew from their lives and personal and professional obligations. Some people lost the ability to function and were never again able to regain anything even remotely resembling their former life.

Before we move on to some of the other major changes and consequences of the Black Death, there's something important that should be mentioned: the issue of blame itself. Of course, it's natural to want to understand the origins of something like the Black Death. In fact, doing so is an important part of learning how to prevent something like it from happening again in the future. However, distrusting an entire ethnic group or reacting violently toward others is never an appropriate response.

Rise of Antisemitism

The surge of antisemitism and authorities' response to it set a dangerous precedent for the years to come. Instances of antisemitism had already been growing across Europe prior to the start of the pandemic, but it increased dramatically once the disease took hold.

As has already been mentioned, many people simply used the Black Death as an excuse to scapegoat the Jewish community and enact their hatred without consequence. And for many, there were no consequences for their actions.

While some authorities spoke out against the mistreatment and killing of Jews, there were many others who stood idly by. Sometimes, government officials and church leaders would even encourage the attacks.

In a study conducted by Finley and Koyama, it was found that attacks on the Jewish community were much more severe in cities that were governed by Catholic leaders. In those cities, Jews were often killed in extremely high numbers. Sometimes, their population would be completely eliminated.

Cities that were ruled by a secular leader saw much lower persecution rates, which speaks loudly to the vendetta the Catholics had against the Jews.

This general ambivalence or blatant encouragement of the massacre of the Jewish people set the stage for future antisemitic attacks. Left unchecked, this eventually led to the attempted genocide of the Jewish people by the Nazis in World War II. By the end of the war, six million Jews had been murdered.

During the most recent pandemic, the same lie was spread regarding the Jewish community, that they had somehow designed and spread the disease with the aim of growing their own population. Since then, the world has observed a spike in antisemitic hate crimes. Despite our incredible access to world events and history, we seem to be continually doomed to repeat our past mistakes. That's why it's so important to continue to learn and spread knowledge.

Inflation and Labor

As is common with most pandemics, the aftermath saw increased rates of inflation. The stalling of every trade system made goods much more difficult and expensive to acquire, and the loss of workers also made the cost of labor go up. This created intense frustration for the upper class, but the higher cost of labor eventually ended up changing the fabric of society.

Europe had previously operated under a feudal system, with a clear separation between lords and their serfs. Higher pay suddenly raised many former peasants to a different level of society, and the middle class was born.

As more and more people began to make a decent living, there was a surge in demand for products that might have been unattainable to laborers before. Even with inflation, people were eager to spend their hard-earned money. After all, there had been very little to celebrate for many years, and in between waves of the plague, people did their best to enjoy what life had to offer.

The creation of the middle class was instrumental in helping the economy recover, as well as providing a better quality of life to a large part of the population. Had the Black Death not happened, there is no telling how long the feudal system might have remained in place.

For a long time, the middle class was a level of wealth that many people aspired to enjoy. This was because people in the middle class generally lived comfortable and happy lives. It was common for people in the middle class to secure a comfortable job and be able to afford a home and the occasional comfort or indulgence.

The middle class expanded for many years. In the 1970s, adults in the middle class in the United States sat at 61 percent. However, over the last twenty years, that number has fallen. The percentage sat at 50 percent in 2021. Of course, this means that the upper class has grown, but it also means the lower class has expanded as well.

A stark divide between the upper and lower classes is a phenomenon that has happened in other countries around the world as well. Currently, there are several attacks on unions and labor protections and regulations all over the world. Many people have to hold several jobs to make ends meet and are being priced out of major cities. Steady, tenured jobs are often being replaced by gig work with no stability or pensions. However, a lot of the massive labor changes that took place after the first wave of the

Black Death took several years, in some cases decades, to organize. Looking back at what happened in the 1300s can perhaps shine a light on what the future might hold for us.

Safety

One thing is certain: The Black Death made the world a safer place. The extreme nature of the disease forced authorities to make massive changes to the way buildings, cities, and healthcare facilities were designed. It also helped create many safe food practices and water purification systems.

Of course, these advancements were not all a direct result of the Black Death, but many of the investigations and experiments that led to these advancements began because of a desperate desire to stem the spread of the plague. These changes to society not only improved the quality of life for survivors but also extended it. And these changes continued to improve over time. Today, many of us are privileged to live in cities that have advanced systems to treat and process food and water. We also have state-of-the-art laboratories, hospitals, and schools that are constantly working to better understand infectious diseases so that we can catch and deal with them as soon as they appear.

Politics

The final area that we'll cover in this chapter is how the Black Death changed politics.

When the Black Death drastically affected the labor market, it meant there was also a shift in the political landscape. Before the arrival of the bubonic plague, many of the lowest-earning members of society had been disenfranchised and did not have much power in the political system.

While political systems might have remained fairly unchanged in areas that didn't experience extremely high death tolls, there was a dramatic shift in areas that had. This created a shift in labor and introduced the middle class. These newly elevated members of society suddenly had a voice in politics and were able to take positions of power, as well as vote for officials that they actually felt would act in their best interest. Prior to the Black Death, politics had been controlled by the elite members of the upper class, who, of course, worked hard to continue the exploitative practices of the feudal system.

This shift in politics created a stronger balance between opposing views and eventually led to party systems, which are common in many countries all over the world today.

In an interview with Gingerich and Vogler, it was discussed how political change was much slower in regions that hadn't experienced high death tolls. Feudal systems were more rigorously protected in these areas, and voter suppression among conservative leaders ran rampant. Land inequality in areas with a lot of loss greatly diminished, and the overall quality of life for everyone in those areas improved.

Of course, these researchers considered the obvious differences in loss of life in different areas due to density differences between rural and urban situations. In general, it was common for rural areas to have better outcomes when it came to deaths simply because there were fewer people to spread the disease. Rural areas had a more dispersed population, which meant better ventilation and pre-established social distancing. However, the trade-off for these areas seemed to be that they took longer to catch up to positive social and economic changes after the first wave of the plague died down.

Despite the fact that some regions progressed more slowly than others, it is an indisputable fact that the Black Death changed the face of politics forever.

There are numerous social and economic changes that happened as a result of the Black Death. Some have been extensively studied, while others have been lost and forgotten to time. Once again, these issues provide a valuable lesson from which we can hopefully learn in order to prevent the same mistakes from happening in the future.

Conclusion

No one wants to imagine the worst-case scenario. The Black Death was a horrific event that permanently changed the course of history. There are so many people who never got to live out their dreams because of this disease. Who knows what art, scientific discoveries, and social advancements we might have had so much earlier had the Black Death never happened. But there's another valid question to ask that's the opposite of that. How much later would we have had some of these things if it hadn't happened?

Would there have been such an intense interest in bacteria and the origin of disease if the Black Death hadn't happened? Would democracy be the same if it hadn't happened? Would we still be operating under a feudal system?

While some of these questions may seem laughable, they are not entirely ridiculous. In this book, there have been several examples of how history has repeated itself after similar traumas, even though there are so many resources that detail how those same choices ended before. Sometimes, the only thing that can really shake up a society and create meaningful change is a catastrophic event like the bubonic plague.

That's not to say that a pandemic is the only way to change the status quo. There have been many movements throughout history that have managed to change long-entrenched social systems through grassroots organizations and a strong passion for the cause. But it's undeniable that the Black Death resulted in some major positive changes.

Even now, many populations around the world, including the United States, live within a system that is predominantly controlled by a wealthy few. Those in the highest tax bracket generally hold the most powerful positions in politics, control think tanks and global corporations, and control the cost of living and wages. Is it a stretch to imagine that some of these politicians and CEOs might comfortably operate within a feudal system if given the chance?

And what would healthcare look like today without the impact of the Black Death? Although there were several other diseases that caused widespread death, there was nothing as severe as the bubonic plague. Is it possible that the loss of life from other ailments wouldn't have been deemed devastating enough to initiate further investigation?

Without the discovery of germ theory, we might still be sitting beside sewage in the hopes of warding off disease. That might not be difficult because we might still be throwing our waste onto the street. Again, this might seem silly and a bit difficult to imagine, but remember that humans can be slow to change and often repeat previous mistakes. Looking back at the 1918 Spanish flu pandemic, it might seem impossible that anyone would have negative reactions to basic public health measures, which people resisted back then. And the same argument appeared again about one hundred years later.

The Black Death showed us that pandemics are quick to fuel animosity and hatred. They stoke powerlessness and hopelessness, and people often turn to anger and extremist views when faced with these feelings. The long history of this pattern can help us learn how to have more measured responses to tragic events such as this. Because another thing the Black Death has taught us is that pandemics will keep on coming. However, it's up to us to decide how we respond to them.

The fear and isolation that happen as a result of a pandemic is detrimental to our health and society at large. In order to create a better world, we need to move forward to embrace curiosity and compassion because there usually is something better on the other side.

If you enjoyed this book, a review on Amazon would be greatly appreciated because it would mean a lot to hear from you.

To leave a review:

1. Open your camera app.
2. Point your mobile device at the QR code.
3. The review page will appear in your web browser.

Thanks for your support!

Here's another book by Enthralling History that you might like

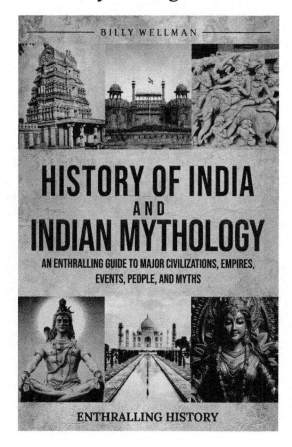

Free limited time bonus

Stop for a moment. We have a free bonus set up for you. The problem is this: we forget 90% of everything that we read after 7 days. Crazy fact, right? Here's the solution: we've created a printable, 1-page pdf summary for this book that you're reading now. All you have to do to get your free pdf summary is to go to the following website:

https://livetolearn.lpages.co/enthrallinghistory/

Once you do, it will be intuitive. Enjoy, and thank you!

Bibliography

Christian, David. "Silk Roads or Steppe Roads?"
https://www.jstor.org/stable/20078816.

Torr, Geordie. *The Silk Roads: A History of the Great Trading Routes Between East and West.*

"Ancient Tea and Horse Caravan Road."
http://www.silkroadfoundation.org/newsletter/2004vol2num1/tea.htm.

"Ancient Tea Horse Road." https://www.bbc.com/travel/article/20120830-asias-ancient-tea-horse-road.

Fan Ye. *Hou Hanshu* (*Book of the Later Han*).

"Trade under the Tang Dynasty."

https://courses.lumenlearning.com/suny-hccc-worldcivilization/chapter/trade-under-the-tang-dynasty/.

"The Prosperity of the Silk Road in the Tang Dynasty."

http://en.shaanxi.gov.cn/as/hac/hos/201704/t20170428_1595517.html.

"Silk Road Overland Transportation." http://www.historyshistories.com/silk-road-transportation-overland-route.html.

"Transportation Along the Silk Road."
http://www.silkroadtourcn.com/blog/160.html.

"Caravans." https://factsanddetails.com/china/cat2/sub90/item1103.html.

"Slave Trade on the Silk Road." https://shanghai.nyu.edu/news/exploring-silk-road-slave-trade-turfan.

Herodotus. *Histories.*

"Ibn Battuta." https://www.khanacademy.org/humanities/big-history-project/expansion-interconnection/exploration-interconnection/a/ibn-battuta.

"Palmyra." https://en.unesco.org/silkroad/content/palmyra.

"Cosmopolitan Silk Road." https://academic.oup.com/isagsq/article/2/1/ksac007/6556077.

"A Journey of Discovery | Smithsonian Folklife Festival." https://festival.si.edu/2002/the-silk-road/a-journey-of-discovery/smithsonian.

"Intangible Cultural Heritage." https://en.unesco.org/silkroad/silk-road-themes/intangible-cultural-heritage.

"Discovering the Islamic architecture of the Silk Road - Saga." https://www.saga.co.uk/magazine/travel/destinations/asia/central-asia/silk-road-islamic-architecture

"CHRISTIANITY, NESTORIANS AND THE SILK ROAD" https://factsanddetails.com/china/cat2/sub90/entry-8324.html

"How Islam got to the Philippines." https://slate.com/news-and-politics/2005/01/how-islam-got-to-the-philippines.html

"Islam in the Philippines - Wikipedia." https://en.wikipedia.org/wiki/Islam_in_the_Philippines

"Islam in China | Pew Research Center." https://www.pewresearch.org/religion/2023/08/30/islam/#:~:text=Islam%20was%20brought%20to%20China,Islam%20began%20to%20spread%20inland.

"Democritus - World History Encyclopedia." https://www.worldhistory.org/Democritus/.

"Alchemy | Encyclopedia.com." https://www.encyclopedia.com/philosophy-and-religion/other-religious-beliefs-and-general-terms/miscellaneous-religion/alchemy.

"Inventions and Trade: The Silk and Spice Routes, 1994." https://en.unesco.org/silkroad/sites/default/files/knowledge-bank-article/ways%20of%20scientific%20exchange.pdf.

"UNESCO in Brief." https://www.unesco.org/en/brief

https://study.com/learn/lesson/the-four-humors-blood-phlegm-black-bile-yellow-bile.html

https://www.folger.edu/blogs/shakespeare-and-beyond/the-four-humors-eating-in-the-renaissance/

https://curiosity.lib.harvard.edu/contagion/feature/humoral-theory

http://exhibits.usu.edu/exhibits/show/bookofsecretes/medicine

https://www.tehrantimes.com/news/415195/Sanguine-temperament-Specifications-and-lifestyle

https://www.worldhistory.org/article/1540/medieval-cures-for-the-black-death/
https://bcmj.org/premise/history-bloodletting
https://www.popularmechanics.com/science/a32759535/newton-toad-vomit-plague-cure/
https://www.sciencedirect.com/science/article/pii/S0378874121007649
https://www.oxfordreference.com/display/10.1093/oi/authority.20110803100046308;jsessionid=8FE8751E77C563B813D981AD9A6BA156
 https://www.businessinsider.com/labor-shortage-history-black-death-plague-king-pay-increase-serfdom-2021-12
https://www.historic-uk.com/HistoryUK/HistoryofEngland/Wat-Tyler-the-Peasants-Revolt/
https://artincontext.org/black-death-art/
https://www.montana.edu/historybug/yersiniaessays/medrano.html#:~:text=The%20trauma%20of%20the%20Black,then%20poetized%2C%20and%20finally%20painted.
https://momentmag.com/why-were-jews-blamed-for-the-black-death/
https://www.worldhistory.org/article/1541/religious-responses-to-the-black-death/
https://www.britannica.com/event/Western-Schism
https://www.historicmysteries.com/avignon-captivity/
https://www.britannica.com/event/Avignon-papacy
https://jewishreviewofbooks.com/articles/9866/jews-genes-and-the-black-death/#
https://source.colostate.edu/penance-and-plague-how-the-black-death-changed-one-of-christianitys-most-important-rituals/
http://web.stanford.edu/class/history13/Readings/MichaelDol.htm#:~:text=The%20Muslim%20reaction%20to%20the,mass%20funerals%20in%20the%20mosques.
https://knowledge.uchicago.edu/record/3111?ln=en
https://egrove.olemiss.edu/cgi/viewcontent.cgi?article=1682&context=hon_thesis
https://www.worldhistory.org/article/1541/religious-responses-to-the-black-death/
https://www.ncbi.nlm.nih.gov/pmc/articles/PMC9949692/
https://academic.oup.com/jsh/article/45/3/809/1746067
https://www.history.com/news/quarantine-black-death-medieval
https://time.com/5799525/coronavirus-covid19-quarantine-ships-history/
https://bigthink.com/health/what-ended-the-black-death-historys-worst-pandemic/#:~:text=The%20eventual%20weakening%20of%20the,slowing%20the%20plague's%20terror%20march.
https://www.history.com/news/pandemics-end-plague-cholera-black-death-smallpox
https://www.britannica.com/biography/Sir-John-Pringle-1st-Baronet
https://health.mil/News/Articles/2021/07/01/Evolution-MHS-MSMR
https://www.wearewater.org/en/sewage-the-trace-of-our-history_281141

https://taras.org/2020/10/10/a-short-history-of-solid-waste-management/#:~:text=Centuries%20with%20no%20organized%20waste,garbage%20was%20a%20common%20practice.

https://education.nationalgeographic.org/resource/natural-selection/

https://www.nih.gov/news-events/nih-research-matters/how-black-death-shaped-human-evolution#:~:text=Researchers%20identified%20genetic%20variants%20that,increasing%20susceptibility%20to%20autoimmune%20diseases.

https://journals.sagepub.com/doi/full/10.1177/18344909211034257

https://sphweb.bumc.bu.edu/otlt/mph-modules/ph/publichealthhistory/publichealthhistory7.html

https://www.thelancet.com/journals/lancet/article/PIIS0140-6736(15)61231-4/fulltext

https://www.britannica.com/topic/feudalism

https://egrove.olemiss.edu/cgi/viewcontent.cgi?article=1682&context=hon_thesis#:~:text=When%20the%20Black%20Death%20struck%20Europe%20in%201347%2C%20the%20increasingly,its%20vulnerability%20to%20Christian%20society.https://dc.cod.edu/cgi/viewcontent.cgi?article=1657&context=essai#:~:text=The%20Greek%20physician%20Hippocrates%20(c,pestilence%20(Sterner%2C%201).

https://www.livescience.com/2497-black-death-changed-world.html

https://www.thehealthy.com/food/why-europeans-dont-refrigerate-eggs/

https://www.cdc.gov/foodsafety/rawmilk/rawmilk-outbreaks.html

https://blog.smartsense.co/louis-pasteur-pasteurization

https://www.britannica.com/story/louis-pasteurs-contributions-to-science#:~:text=Pasteur's%20work%20with%20microorganisms%20in,of%20the%20body%20by%20microorganisms.

https://www.ncbi.nlm.nih.gov/pmc/articles/PMC3940030/#:~:text=Acetic%20acid%20(vinegar)%20is%20an,disinfectant%20capacity%20of%20organic%20acids.

https://bio.libretexts.org/Bookshelves/Microbiology/Microbiology_(Boundless)/10%3A_Epidemiology/10.01%3A_Principles_of_Epidemiology/10.1A%3A_History_of_Epidemiology

https://www.thelancet.com/journals/lancet/article/PIIS0140-6736(06)69878-4/fulltext

https://www.cdc.gov/vaccines/vpd/vaccines-diseases.html

https://www.who.int/news-room/spotlight/history-of-vaccination/a-brief-history-of-vaccination#:~:text=Dr%20Edward%20Jenner%20created%20the,cowpox%20were%20immune%20to%20smallpox.&text=In%20May%201796%2C%20English%20physician,the%20hand%20of%20a%20milkmaid.

https://www.vbivaccines.com/evlp-platform/louis-pasteur-attenuated-vaccine/

https://sciencehistory.org/education/scientific-biographies/louis-pasteur/#:~:text=During%20the%20mid%2D%20to%20late,cholera%2C%20anthrax%2C%20and%20rabies.

https://www.sciencefocus.com/the-human-body/epidemiology-a-timeline-of-discoveries/

https://www.aaas.org/discovery-bacteria#:~:text=Two%20men%20are%20credited%20today,discovery%20of%20bacteria%20in%201676.

https://curiosity.lib.harvard.edu/contagion/feature/germ-theory

https://www.pasteur.fr/en/research-journal/news/alexandre-yersin-man-who-discovered-bacterium-responsible-plague

https://www.cnn.com/2020/08/19/health/bubonic-plague-2020-california-wellness/index.html

https://www.healthline.com/health-news/seriously-dont-worry-about-the-plague#Heres-how-the-plague-spreads

https://www.nature.com/articles/s41586-022-04800-3

https://www.science.org/content/article/gene-helped-people-survive-black-death-come-haunt#:~:text=The%20team%20identified%20an%20astonishing,called%20endoplasmic%20reticulum%20aminopeptidase%202.

https://www.sciencedirect.com/science/article/pii/S1198743X14608582

https://www.ncbi.nlm.nih.gov/books/NBK218224/

https://www.unco.edu/assault-survivors-advocacy-program/learn_more/neurobiology_of_trauma.aspx#:~:text=When%20someone%20experiences%20a%20traumatic,all%20have%20inside%20of%20us.

https://www.wvdhhr.org/birth23/raunewsletters/RAU7_Summer2018_PPNewsletter.pdf

https://pdxscholar.library.pdx.edu/cgi/viewcontent.cgi?article=1197&context=younghistorians#:~:text=The%20absence%20of%20reassurance%20that,on%20the%20function%20of%20society.

https://jogh.org/2022/jogh-12-03015

https://www.pewresearch.org/short-reads/2022/04/20/how-the-american-middle-class-has-changed-in-the-past-five-decades/

https://www.khanacademy.org/humanities/whp-origins/era-5-the-first-global-age/52-old-world-webs-betaa/a/read-trade-networks-and-the-black-death-beta

https://www.brown.edu/Departments/Italian_Studies/dweb/plague/effects/social.php#:~:text=Since%20it%20was%20so%20difficult,the%20new%20rise%20in%20wages.

https://www2.gwu.edu/~iiep/assets/docs/papers/2020WP/JedwabIIEP2020-14.pdf

https://www.ohchr.org/en/press-releases/2020/04/rise-antisemitic-hatred-during-covid-19-must-be-countered-tougher-measures

https://news.virginia.edu/content/qa-new-research-reveals-political-changes-wrought-black-death

https://www.ncbi.nlm.nih.gov/books/NBK218224/

https://www.ncbi.nlm.nih.gov/pmc/articles/PMC3559034/

https://www.history.com/news/quarantine-black-death-medieval#
https://www.sciencemuseum.org.uk/objects-and-stories/medicine/bubonic-plague-first-pandemic
https://education.nationalgeographic.org/resource/silk-road/
https://www.worldhistory.org/article/1540/medieval-cures-for-the-black-death/
https://www.nytimes.com/2022/06/15/health/black-death-plague.html#:~:text=Historians%20traced%20the%20epidemic's%20path,Africa%20and%20the%20Middle%20East.
https://www.nationalgeographic.com/history/article/plague-doctors-beaked-masks-coronavirus